W9-AMX-097

THE WORLD OF WILLIAM FAULKNER

THE WORLD
OF
WILLIAM FAULKNER

WARD L. MINER

PAGEANT BOOK CO. NEW YORK

1959

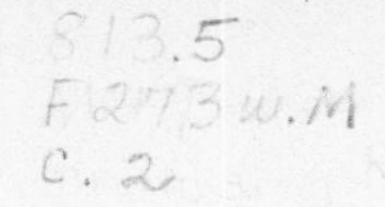

Originally published by Duke University Press

Library of Congress Catalog Card No. 59-8274

Published By Pageant Book Co.
59 Fourth Avenue, New York 3, N. Y.

MANUFACTURED IN THE UNITED STATES OF AMERICA

TABLE OF CONTENTS

ACKNOWLEDGMENTS

It is a pleasure to thank the many people, both named and unnamed, who have contributed their time and energy to make this study possible. Especially I wish to thank Professor Sculley Bradley of the University of Pennsylvania for his innumerable courtesies, unfailing kindnesses, and suggestive criticisms. The implications of the editing of The Portable Faulkner *by Malcolm Cowley have undoubtedly contributed much in clarifying my thinking about Faulkner and his Saga. Within the town of Oxford, Mississippi, there are many people whom I shall always remember for their courteous hospitality and patient answering of questions. I especially appreciate their kindness because frequently I was not even clear in my own mind just what I wanted and was fumbling in self-created fogs. Particularly though I want to thank Phil Stone of Oxford, to whom all readers of Faulkner should be grateful. At a time when everybody, including publishers, was ignoring the young William Faulkner, Phil Stone maintained his faith and confidence in the ultimate worth of what Faulkner was doing. Also, the assistance of the reference staff of the Temple University Library has been an invaluable asset and one greatly appreciated. Finally, the sheer drudgery that my wife, Thelma, has undertaken has meant more than these few words can indicate.*

The final copy for the printer has been prepared in Paris, where I have not been able to reverify many of my quotations and data. For errors I ask the reader's indulgence.

WARD L. MINER.
Paris, France, 1952.

CREDITS

Grateful acknowledgments are due the following publishers for permission to quote from the works listed below:

To Random House, Inc., for the quotations from the various books by Faulkner;

To the *American Mercury* for the quotation from William Faulkner's "Folklore of the Air";

To Harcourt, Brace and Company, Inc., for the quotation from Alfred Kazin's *On Native Grounds* (copyright, 1942, by Alfred Kazin);

To Hastings House, Inc., for quotations from the *Mississippi State Guide (Mississippi: A Guide to the Magnolia State).*

Of the several unpublished studies used herein, mention should be made of John C. Hathorn's master's thesis, "A Period Study of Lafayette County from 1836 to 1860 with Emphasis on Population Groups" (University of Mississippi, 1939).

I

TWO SMALL TOWNS

During the summer of 1949 I spent some time in two small towns. One is Oxford, Mississippi; the other, Mount Pleasant, Iowa. That summer certain basic similarities struck me. Both communities were founded in the 1830's; both are county seats in a rural environment; both have hundred-year-old colleges in or near the towns (Oxford's is the state university; the other's is a small denominational college); and both reached their peaks in community vigor during the period immediately preceding the Civil War. So much alike, yet the spirit brooding over the two places is very much different.

Many times since then I have asked myself why. Why should two rural communities of somewhat similar frontier experiences and histories be so fundamentally different? An easy answer is to say that one is in Mississippi and the other in Iowa. The South and the Midwest are not the same, and that difference is basic to the answer to my question, though not all the answer.

Walking the streets of Oxford, I found myself remembering my own boyhood in Iowa and comparing my memories with what I could observe of the lives of the children about me. In common with them I grew up hearing much talk about the prospects for corn. They would have heard about cotton and I could remember leisurely gossip on wheat and oats, but the difference in mood would not have been great. As a boy I helped farmers with haying, threshing, and other farm jobs. I'm sure a boy in Oxford from an economic background similar to mine would have spent his summers in much the same way I did. That indefinable quality called rural brings the two communities together.

Strolling under the trees of Oxford, I thought in more particular terms of my childhood. One important day — my eighth birthday, I believe — I got my first borrower's card from the local library ; I could charge out books in my own name and not have to ask an older brother or sister to get them for me. I buried myself in the wonders of Thornton W. Burgess's animal stories and in the "boy's life" of this or that person. I learned, albeit I was unaware of the process, to love books and to appreciate their possibilities. Today I realize I was partaking of the New England tradition, transplanted to the Midwest, which assumes a free library must be available for the townspeople, whether of eight or eighty years.

Oxford — no, Oxford has no town library. The children of Oxford would not have the thrill I had. That New England spirit, so vital in the southeast Iowa community, is not active in Oxford. It is the presence or absence of this tradition that is more important than the location — South or Midwest.

If Oxford does not have the New England tradition, it does have pronounced traditions of its own. I thought about that as I walked along Oxford's streets late at night after just about all the citizens had gone to bed and the lights in the houses were out and the second movie had ended. The traditions are different, yes, but there is something else different and even peculiar to Oxford. It is the attitude towards these traditions. These attitudes result in a physical distinction between Oxford and my boyhood town in Iowa. The Iowa community is going through a spasm of home building and remodelling. Old houses are being repainted. But in Oxford the old houses are just standing. A few new homes are being built and some are frequently and tastefully repainted, but many are not. After people had turned off their house lights and midnight had passed, I could still sense the presence in Oxford of a miasma-like past pervading the town. This past seemed to have an existence all its own, entirely independent of the town's inhabitants, who are in so many ways, I noticed in the daytime, dependent upon that past. Therein lay the real difference between Oxford, Mississippi, and Mount Pleasant, Iowa.

The particular distinction, for me, of Oxford is its most famous citizen, William C. Faulkner. His works, centering as they do upon a fictitious, though typical, Mississippi town called "Jefferson," reveal a study of decadence through many generations, unsurpassed in contemporary writing. Jefferson kept me in Oxford, even during the heat of the summer, because I realized that, if I could learn about Oxford, its traditions and its way of life, I could undoubtedly better understand the meaning of the life in fictitious Jefferson.

The theme for this study is the Yoknapatawpha

Saga. The setting for the Saga is a legendary county in northwest Mississippi — Yoknapatawpha — but its actual prototype is Lafayette county, whose county seat is Oxford. An understanding of the Saga, which includes most of Faulkner's works, clarifies also the meaning of those other works that lie outside its limits. A mere listing of the books directly using the Yoknapatawpha setting shows how important the Saga is for any reader of Faulkner: *Sartoris; The Sound and the Fury; As I Lay Dying; Sanctuary; These 13* (short stories, some of which are set in Yoknapatawpha county); *Light in August; Doctor Martino and Other Stories* (more short stories with varied settings); *Absalom, Absalom!; The Unvanquished; The Hamlet; Go Down, Moses and Other Stories* (all set in this county); *Intruder in the Dust; Knight's Gambit; Collected Stories of William Faulkner;* and *Requiem for a Nun.* In addition to all of *These 13* and most of *Doctor Martino,* the *Collected Stories* contains many stories available earlier only in various magazines, most of which are also set in the fictional county. Other books deal with localities not far from northwest Mississippi and have an indirect relationship to the county, because, of course, Yoknapatawpha county does not exist in a cultural or geographic isolation. The "Old Man" story in *The Wild Palms* has its setting on the Mississippi River and in the Mississippi Delta country in the extreme western part of the state. Most of the title story of this volume takes place in New Orleans and on the Mississippi Gulf Coast. The incidents in *Pylon* occur in New Valois, a rather transparent pseudonym for New Orleans. New Orleans and a yachting trip from the city are the scenes for *Mosquitoes.* Aside from fugitive items, this includes all of Faulkner's books except his first novel, *Soldier's Pay,* and his two volumes of poetry. Obviously in quantitative terms Yoknapatawpha county is basic to Faulkner's works; its qualitative importance I hope to demonstrate.

To do so, I must explore the relation between the fictional county and actuality. How does the actuality of Lafayette county and Oxford provide a basis for the legendary reality of Yoknapatawpha county with its county seat, Jefferson? With any writer there exists a subtle relationship between the world from which he derives his being and sustenance and the world he creates in his imagination. The world of Yoknapatawpha county is a much more complete and explicit world than the usual writer creates; therefore it is peculiarly appropriate that the subject for this study be the relationships between the worlds of Yoknapatawpha and Lafayette counties — together comprising the world of William Faulkner.

As a result of this definition certain problems will inevitably be omitted or treated very casually. Among these is the biography of the man, William C. Faulkner, who was born in New Albany, Mississippi, in 1897, now resides in Oxford, and has written a series of books. Biography is not the concern here, even though it could reveal much about the writer and his works. Neither is the development of the writer, William Faulkner, extending from a small volume of poetry, *The Marble Faun,* in 1924, and some miscellaneous writing for New Orleans newspapers and fugitive magazines in 1925 and 1926, through the steady stream of novels during the 1930's, and up to the present.

A particular problem of Faulkner's technique not treated here is the involved syntax of his sentences. A method of attack might be a study in contrast between the stripped, concentrated sentences of the early Hemingway and the expanded, sometimes diffuse sentences employed by Faulkner. Syntax, use of subordinate elements in the sentence, diction, what is included within the expression "style" — all contrast.

Nor will the literary influences on Faulkner be dwelt on here, unless they are relevant to the study itself. Among these influences are the design of Balzac's Human Comedy, the historical plays of Shakespeare, Sherwood Anderson both as writer and friend, T. S. Eliot's early poetry, Joyce's works and others using similar techniques of stream of consciousness, Swinburne's exotic lushness, and the entire school of naturalists in this country — beginning with Dreiser and Norris.

Much then is still to be written about Faulkner, but I have chosen a subject that, while limited in scope, seems to me to get at the meaningful core of his fiction better than any other possible approach. First I want to give a brief history of the actual town of Oxford and the county of Lafayette (locally this is pronounced with the accent on the second syllable). As much as I can I wish to get at what, for want of a better term, might be called the spirit of the community. In practice this means that names of actual persons in the locality will not be emphasized. Intangibles will be stressed, though not to the exclusion of tangibles which reveal patterns of behavior. In history tangibles have a value only as they have acquired symbolic functions through intimate association with the intangible personalities of men. And the story of Lafayette county is the story of individual personalities acting upon and being acted upon by conditions originating from both within the county and outside it.

I shall attempt a history of the fictitious town of Jefferson and the county of Yoknapatawpha.

Obviously the only source is the novels and stories by Faulkner. Since this is true, we shall have to pry behind the façade of the books to ferret out a more or less chronological sequence. But just as one tries not to deviate from recorded data in writing conventional history, I shall try not to deviate from Yoknapatawpha's recorded data and facts — Faulkner's books.

What will Oxford tell us about Jefferson? How do the legendary town and county derive from the actual ones? What has the imagination of this creative artist done to his source material to make possible the creative values in his books? What historical patterns does Oxford reveal for us in Jefferson?

II

ACTUALITY

Oxford, Mississippi, is a quiet, almost somnolent town located in the northwest part of the state, a little over forty miles from the Tennessee border. The 1950 United States Census gave the town a population of 3,956 and the county of Lafayette, of which Oxford is the county seat, 22,798. Lafayette, with an area of 679 square miles, spreads over the hill country just east of the Mississippi Delta region. A small part of the county's soil is the black, alluvial bottom land found along two rivers, although the building of the Sardis Reservoir has flooded much of the Tallahatchie River bottom land. Most of the soil is the red, relatively poor land found in the rolling hills. The Tallahatchie River forms the eastern half of the county's northern border. The Yocona River (the earliest records of the county and state list this as the "Yocanapatafa" River, with the *f* sometimes written *ph*), flowing also towards the Mississippi, runs just within the county's southern border. Oxford is approximately in the center of the county. Immediately to the west of Oxford is the separately incorporated community, University, which is the University of Mississippi.

There is no need to describe the physical appearance of the town to anyone who has seen the movie version of Faulkner's novel, *Intruder in the Dust*. The white, almost square courthouse, topped by its clock-bearing cupola, broods over the town like a setting hen over her hatching eggs. Most of the business district is located around the courthouse square. In the center of the square to the south of the courthouse is the statue of a Confederate soldier so common in Southern communities. The inscription on the pedestal honors those who died "in a just and holy cause." One of the first things that a visitor (locally he is called an outlander) notices is the cleanliness of the town.

The second and more lasting impression than the cleanliness, and somehow the first impression becomes part of the second, is that of decay — ultra-respectable and genteel, but still decay. This decay includes the very land itself, gashed by the gullies of continual erosion. Though the gullies are not as deep as they were in the 1920's and many are covered over with Kudzu vine, they are still very much there. Like the land, the people in the community have been gullied by a spiritual decay, though covered over with a veneer of respectability. Families once bold and vigorous are now spectators rather than participating actors.

What produced this decay? What wasted not only the soil of this county but the minds of these people? Why do all civilizations decay? We do not yet know. But the comprehension of what is involved in the decay of a small community such as Oxford should contribute to the comprehension of why large civilizations decay. Why are large cultural patterns swallowed and, as it were, discarded by peoples?

Mississippi became a state in 1817, but her history goes back long before that date. Many forces, produced both by man and nature, had been active for many years. Nature gives man, no matter where, certain materials with which to work. We must, in perceiving a region in its entirety, recognize what nature has given man. For Lafayette county a meaningful beginning of its story is the epoch of water. Water — what preceded the present Gulf of Mexico — covered the state of Mississippi until a time relatively recent for a geologist. The water slowly receded, leaving the present soil mostly alluvial in origin. The bluffs east of the Mississippi River owe part of their existence to the wind which carried material from the deposits of the flood waters of glaciers to the north. But the sea was the primary factor in the formation of the soil.

The all-important geographic element is the Mississippi River, even though the county's western borders are between forty-five and sixty miles from the river. All streams eventually pour into this river, and it is both a physical and psychological force in the lives of all Mississippians. The geographic structure of the county, already briefly sketched, includes the two streams whose waters empty into the all-encompassing "father of waters." The Mississippi River not only drains the land but also draws to itself the minds of the people.

The climate is, of course, relatively warm in summer, but rainy and chilly in winter. The nights are cooler during the summer than might be expected so far from the Gulf coast, perhaps because the elevation is above that of the hot, humid Delta. But the days are warm enough to produce a chronic lethargy.

Man enters into our story with the Indians and with their predecessors, the mound-builders. There are still to be found a few small mounds scattered over Lafayette county. The Indian tribe to have lived most recently in this county was the Chickasaw. The Chickasaws were related to their neighbors, the Choctaws, and both tribes were present when de Soto in 1540 entered what is now the state of Mississippi. The cultural effect of the Chickasaws upon the mores and folkways of the present inhabitants of Lafayette county is probably not large; still they did have an influence over and beyond their naming of rivers and hills.

Let me give a particular example of this intangible influence. In Mississippi the last Indian land cession was made by the Chickasaws in 1832. In 1837 a Chickasaw woman sued in the courts of the state of Mississippi for her property, then claimed by her husband. Under Chickasaw law wives had property rights separate from those of their husbands. The woman won her case because the court declared that the marriage and the acquiring of the property had taken place before 1832 while the couple were still under tribal law. In 1839 the Mississippi legislature passed a law granting separate property rights to all free married women of the state.[1] Today this law is a commonplace in almost all states but then it was a rarity. This story well illustrates the kind of influence the Indians had — in details rather than in general patterns, although their physical prowess, of course, became imbedded in the legends for children.

1. John F. H. Claiborne, *Mississippi as a Province, Territory and State* (Jackson, Mississippi, 1880), p. 475.

Romantic notions of the "noble savage" survived also, but there was much more than this. Mississippi folklore preserves tales of the cruelty of the Indians, of customs that to the whites seemed inexplicable, and of the pride of the white men who boasted that "the only good Indian was a dead Indian." Folklore blended together the Indian and the frontier, as actual history had already done.

Between 1832 and 1835 the Chickasaws moved from Mississippi to the Indian Territory (Oklahoma) but there were a few who remained. In the northwest of Lafayette county there is to be found a small creek named Tobitubby or Tobytubby. *Toby* means "old" or "bent," and *Tubby* or *tubbe* means "chief."

> This little tributary of the Tallahatchie River is named for an old Indian Chief named the Toby who lived here when treaty [Pontotoc Creek treaty in 1832, which sent the Chickasaws to Oklahoma] was signed. It is said that he was very wealthy and owned many slaves. When he died, a slave was selected to be buried with him, but some white people heard of the plan and prevented it.[2]

It should be added that for many years, "the Toby," or "Toby Tubby" as he usually was called, ran a ferry on the Memphis-Oxford stage coach route near what is now Abbeville.

A Choctaw chieftain after whom the city of Greenwood, Mississippi, is named should also be mentioned here, even though he did not live in Lafayette county, for his reputation in Mississippi was undoubtedly the greatest of all the Indians who remained among the whites. A recent account of him and his house states:

2. Mrs. Minnie Smith Holt, "Oxford, Mississippi," typewritten MS., University of Mississippi Library (1936), p. 25.

This palatial old home [Malmaison] of Greenwood Leflore, last Choctaw chieftain, was built in 1854 as a succession to the log house built by Leflore in 1835. Named for the home in which the Empress Josephine found refuge after her divorce from Napoleon, the house shows both French and Southern colonial influence in its architecture. It is a two-story white frame structure with massive grooved columns on the porticos. Long narrow galleries extend the length of the house on both sides. Irregularly placed are iron grillwork balconies. On the roof is an observatory enclosed by elaborately designed iron railings. From here Leflore's beloved Teoc (Ind. *place of tall pines*) country is visible for miles.

Fourteen immense rooms, seven on each floor, open off the wide hallways that cross in the center of the house. Their furnishings were designed for Leflore by Parisian decorators. In the parlor is a Louis XIV suite finished in gold leaf and upholstered in rich red brocaded damask. On the walls large gold-framed mirrors alternate with murals of French and Swiss scenes. On the linen curtains are painted pictures of the French palaces, Malmaison, St. Cloud, Fountainebleau, and Versailles. The library contains portraits of Colonel Leflore, his wife, and daughter. Beneath the portrait of Leflore hang a sword and bell presented to him by the U. S. Government upon his election as Chief of the Choctaw.

Greenwood Leflore, the son of Louis Le Fleur, French trader and trapper..., and Rebecca Crevat, niece of Pushmataha, was born at Le Fleur's Bluff (now Jackson) in 1800 and named for an English sea-captain. He was adopted by Maj. John Donley, who owned a stage line on the Natchez Trace, and was educated in Nashville. In 1819 he married the major's daughter Rose and returned with her to Mississippi shortly afterward. In 1824, when for the first time a Choctaw chief was chosen by general election, the honor went to Leflore. He effected many reforms among his people, notable among which was the abolition of witchcraft practices and the establishment of schools for Indian children. For 10 years Leflore was tireless in his efforts to raise the standards of living among the Choctaw. He

> was in his thirties, tall, handsome, and at the height of his power, when a conference was called at Dancing Rabbit Creek to decide upon the sale of Choctaw lands to the United States. ... Because he realized that the treaty was inevitable and sponsored it, Leflore was condemned as a traitor by his tribe. It was through his influence, however, that an amendment was added whereby an Indian who desired to remain in the State received a section of land and enjoyed full protection of the government. Leflore, after the removal of a majority of the Choctaw, lost face with the remaining members of his tribe. His later prestige came entirely from his standing with white men. As a cotton planter he prospered greatly during the period 1840-60. He was elected to the lower house of the State legislature in 1835 and to the Senate in 1844. For his third wife, Priscilla Donley, sister of Rose Donley, he built Malmaison, expressing in it both his Indian love of display and his planter wealth. Leading to Malmaison was a clay and cinder road, the first attempted hard-surfacing of a road in the State. With the outbreak of the War between the States, Leflore was ostracized by Indians and Southern whites alike. He refused to give up his United States citizenship and to support the Confederacy, and an attack was made on his life by Confederates; at another time a fire of incendiary origin broke out at Malmaison. When he died, August 21, 1865, he was wrapped for burial in the flag he loved and interred on a hillside near Malmaison.[3]

The United States Bureau of the Census report for 1860 lists no Indians in Lafayette county. Whatever influence they had as a result of living among the white population of the county must then be dated before 1860. Actually by 1839 almost all of them were out of the county and in the Indian Territory. As the story of Leflore

3. Federal Writers' Project, *Mississippi: a Guide to the Magnolia State* (New York, 1938), pp. 403-5.

illustrates, however, the Indian in this region helped to preserve some French influences.

The first white settlements were made by the French along the Mississippi River, starting at what is now Natchez and extending on down the river to New Orleans. Though few people in France benefited from John Law's Mississippi Bubble, there was an increase in the number of settlers in this fertile region. Large plantations were developed, men finding the means of getting rich. Slaves were introduced and used extensively by these early planters of tobacco and indigo. By 1817 these planters were well established and in a position to run the political machinery of the new state just as they had that of the territory. These ruling planters were conservatives and formed the nucleus of the later Whig party. They tried to maintain close relations with the Whigs of the North, especially those in commercial and banking circles.

But after 1817 an element of political opposition appeared. When Mississippi was made a state, its northern two-thirds was controlled and occupied by the Indians. Between 1820 and 1832 a series of treaties sent the Indians (as has been indicated) into the Indian Territory and opened the entire state to white settlers. The people from adjacent states who pushed into this area were Jacksonian Democrats. These newcomers had their fortunes yet to make. So there was the inevitable conflict between those on the make and those already made. As in so many parts of the nation, and in the national government itself, this struggle involved a fight over the banking situation. In 1836 and 1837 the Democrats won political control of the state and rarely lost it before the Civil War. In 1844 the Democrats coordinated their control by reapportioning the state counting only the whites. The so-called "federal population" figures, in use before, had counted each slave as three-fifths of one white person.[4] This reapportionment was an effective weapon against the Mississippi Whigs, since the majority of the slaves in the state were on the large plantations near the Mississippi River, and among the owners of these plantations the Whig strength resided.

The influx of settlers during the thirties and forties resulted in "wild-cat" speculation and a turbulence so violent as to become legendary This legend assumed a literary form in the volume of sketches by Joseph G. Baldwin, *The Flush Times of Alabama and Mississippi* (1853) The title gave an appropriate name to the period, though Baldwin may very well have used an expression already current in these states, and the book remains an excellent source for knowledge of the prevailing social conditions.

The "flush times" caused the displacement of the Natchez Whigs as the ruling party of the state, but the political consequences were only one part of a complex pattern, to be found in almost any new territory being opened for settlement. Lawyers had a field day, not only with civil suits over land claims but also with criminal cases resulting from the volatile spirits found in and among those yet-to-be disciplined pioneer citizens. Baldwin was himself one of the many young lawyers who entered such regions, lured by the chance of quick and adventuresome success. Credit was plentiful and everybody appeared to be on the verge of making a fortune. Such communities seemed bent on demonstrating the Darwinian concept of survival of the fittest and were content to let the devil take the hindmost. In Alabama

4. Percy Rainwater, *Mississippi, Storm Center of Secession, 1856-1861* (Baton Rouge, 1938), p. 9.

a fictional rogue of the period summed up the dominant viewpoint, "It is good to be shifty in a new country." [5]

But there is another side of the picture. A rough, turbulent period not only produces shifty characters, but also compels the normally law-abiding people to depend upon a simple and practical moral code, almost universally understood and accepted, rather than upon the more formalized traditions of law and conventional manners. The frontier had its lawless aspect, yes, but it also produced a simple, rough justice that passed into the folkways of pioneer Mississippi and left its mark on modern behavior. Reuben Davis, a member of Congress from Mississippi between 1857 and 1861, in his memoirs described the late 1820's in this fashion:

> People had not begun to write about muscular Christianity in those days, but they understood and practiced it. Their creed was generally simple. A man ought to fear God, and mind his business. He should be respectful and courteous to all women; he should love his friends and hate his enemies. He should eat when he was hungry, drink when he was thirsty, dance when he was merry, vote for the candidate he liked best, and knock down any man who questioned his right to these privileges. [6]

Out of these flush times came most of the leaders of Mississippi through the time of the Civil War. The political leaders of the '50's had been the struggling lawyers of the '30's. Reuben Davis is a good example, and there are very few of the Mississippi leaders of the Confederacy who do not fit into this picture. It is important to

5. Johnson C. Hooper, *Some Adventures of Captain Simon Suggs* (Philadelphia, 1846), p. 12.
6. Reuben Davis, *Recollections of Mississippi and Mississippians* (Boston, 1889), p. 19.

emphasize that most of them, even the so-called "fire-eaters," were social upstarts not born in Mississippi, but attracted by the opportunities of the new state, bringing from the Carolinas, Georgia, Alabama, and Tennessee a mixture of customs and attitudes, together with a spirit of adventure — a combination likely to produce discontent and violence in troubled times.

The story of the town, Oxford, starts in 1835 when John Chisholm, John J. Craig, and John D. Martin opened an Indian trading post near what is now Oxford's square. Robert Shegog and Thomas Dudley Isom (later Dr. Isom) joined them soon afterwards to form the nucleus for the settlement.[7] Within a few months (February 9, 1836) the state legislature passed an act creating Lafayette county.[8] During 1836 the active sale of land in the county started from a federal land office in Pontotoc. It should be noted here that the government, according to the treaty of Pontotoc in 1832, was acting as agent for the Chickasaw Indians in selling the land. Most of the abstracts of land titles in the county therefore have as their first entry a sale from an Indian to a white man. On June 12, 1836, Chisholm, Martin, and Craig bought from Hokah, a Chickasaw woman, land which included within its boundaries what became the town of Oxford.[9] Ten days later, on June 22, 1836, the newly organized county board of police (now the county board of supervisors) officially named Oxford as the county seat and, at the same time, accepted

7. Federal Writers' Project, *Mississippi*, p. 255.
8. John C. Hathorn, *A Period Study of Lafayette County from 1836 to 1860 with Emphasis on Population Groups*, M. A. Thesis, University of Mississippi Library (1939), p. 27.
9. Federal Writers' Project, *Mississippi*, p. 255.

the gift of fifty acres from Martin, Chisholm, and Craig for the site of the town.[10] A year later the town was incorporated. The county and town should be considered as direct developments of the flush times. It is out of these rough, turbulent, hard-drinking, hard-loving times that Oxford sprang. To her came not only land speculators but settlers who would build homes, farms, and stores — the essentials for permanent living.

What were these new settlers like, these transplanted pioneers from Alabama, Tennessee, and the Carolinas? They were not people already either wealthy or well educated. From the old Board of Police Minutes and other old records of the county one can guess that the average county official had not finished the equivalent of grammar school. They were not generally illiterate, but they obviously felt ill at ease in writing the language. The population figures show what would be expected on the frontier. The 1840 census gives the county a population of 3,689 whites, of whom 2,018 were males. Of the males 1,134 were under twenty years of age. The slave census shows a different pattern — 1,412 males and 1,430 females.

The first important event to strike the new community was the Panic of 1837. Many newly hatched schemes for wealth were abandoned overnight. Banks closed and some places in the county never recovered from the effects of the depression. Typical of these was the town of Wyatt, about thirteen miles north of Oxford on the Tallahatchie River. By 1835 Wyatt was a prosperous trading center. Local legends have it that at this time it was a much busier place

10. Hathorn, *Lafayette County,* p. 49. The name, Oxford, was chosen in the hope that the state university would be located there.

than Memphis. Steamboats went between New Orleans and Wyatt, the head of navigation on the Tallahatchie. But Wyatt never got over the Panic. A bank closed, and a Lafayette county phrase for worthless money was "Wyatt money." [11] Oxford survived the bad times, but the going was not easy for a while. Evidence of this is that on February 25, 1839, the county was holding the notes of forty-one men for $33,164 from the sale of town lots in Oxford. [12] Something of the county's difficulties can be seen in the following order from the Minutes of the Board of Police:

> Jan. 16, 1838
> Ordered by the Police Court that all persons indebted to the County of Lafayette for Town lotes in the Town of Oxford by paying half of the instalment due Feby. 15, 1838 shall be endulged for the residue of said instalment untill it passes the next circuit court, persons failing to comply with this order will meet with no indulgence. [13]

A probable effect of the Panic is seen in the installation of a second-floor debtor's room in the county jail, built shortly before the courthouse, even though a state law forbade imprisonment for debt. But by 1840 the worst of the depression was over, helped as the community was by the completion of the courthouse on January 12, 1840, at a cost of $25,100. [14]

One way, perhaps, to give a feeling for this community is to present a series of glimpses into Oxford's social and cultural life. The order of presentation is, of course, unimportant but the

11. Hathorn, *Lafayette County,* p. 42.
12. *Ibid.,* p. 39.
13. Minutes Board of Police, Lafayette County, p. 97.
14. Two contractors, Gordon and Grayson, built the structure. Hathorn, *Lafayette County,* pp. 44-5.

details should accumulate into a whole. To begin — the old county records show that cattle brands were recorded during these years (most likely because of thieving outlaws operating from either the Mississippi River or the old Natchez Trace), and that the public well dug in 1837 on the west side of the square did not satisfy the thirst of the population, since many licenses were issued about this time for taverns, inns, and the like. The following rather cryptic entry also appears:

> 24 April 1837
>
> Ordered that Hiram & James McMilliour be granted a License to keep a house of private entertainment in said town [Oxford] for six months.[15]

One of the first acts of the county board of police in 1836 had been to set up what we today would call price control for inns and taverns. The quality of the accommodations may be questioned, but the prices at least are attractive.

Man and Horse for 24 hours [increased to $3.00 in 1838]	$2.25
All-night supper & breakfast	1.75
All-night, only supper	1.25
Dinner	.50
Supper or breakfast	.37
Lodging	.12½
Single horse all night	.75
Single horse per day	1.12½
Spirits per drink	.12½[16]

The best known local inn was the Oxford Inn, sometimes called the Butler Hotel, advertised as a "large brick mansion."[17] This inn was on the

15. Minutes Board of Police, Lafayette County, p. 55.
16. Hathorn, *Lafayette County,* p. 56.
17. *The Observer* (Oxford), September 16, 1843, p. 1.

site of the present Colonial Hotel. It is interesting to note that the manuscript records of the WPA Lafayette County History, available in the State Archives at Jackson, Mississippi, suggest that the proprietor of the inn, a Captain Butler, was an ancestor of William Faulkner through the line of his grandmother, Mrs. Murray Falkner.

The 1840 census shows that there were thirteen free Negroes in the county. The legal method of coping with them is revealed by the following entry:

> Roda Smith a free negro this day made application for a license to remain in this state. She is rather copper collour common size and about the age of twenty-nine years. She also sustantiated a good character and honest deportment. Whereupon it is ordered by the court that said Roda Smith be granted a license to remain in this state.[18]

It should not be thought that the populace spent all its time in the local bars and "groceries" or "doggeries." The newspapers of Oxford during the 1840's usually had a couple of columns advertising books, chiefly from Philadelphia publishers, but many also from New York. A news item from one of these weekly newspapers tells us something of the community interest in non-material things.

> The Oxford Lyceum. —We forgot to notice in our paper of last Saturday that a public discussion was to take place in this Society on the following Wednesday evening, when a general invitation to all the citizens was intended. The members of this institution meet on every Wednesday evening for exercises. According to the constitution every 4th meeting is to be public

18. Probate Records No. 1, Lafayette County, March 12, 1839, p. 33.

> and a general invitation extended to our citizens to attend, the next public meeting will be on the 15th of next month; the exercises are generally lectures, recitations, critical readings of the British poets, debating and discussion of themes. Our citizens would find it interesting to attend. By the way, we have some promising young orators, not to be sneezed at.[19]

Education was a hit-or-miss affair. There were no publicly supported schools. The private schools, of which there were several in the county, were old-fashioned dame-schools. In 1840 about twenty per cent of the white children of school age in the county were attending school. This percentage did not change much before the Civil War.[20]

Perhaps a specific example of how an individual came to Lafayette county and what he achieved would tell something of the prosperity in the community after the Panic of 1837.

> Alexander Hamilton Pegues, Sr., son of Maladir Pegues and Charlotte Johnson was born June 6, 1808 in Marlborough District, S.C. He removed to Tenn. in 1834 and settled in Lafayette County, Miss. In that part of the county, known as Woodson's Ridge as a young farmer among the Indians, he built his bachelor home of logs. ... The house was about 7½ miles from Oxford. Here they [the family he had by then acquired] lived for many years in great prosperity on a tract of about four thousand acres, and owned 150 slaves at the beginning of the Civil War. ... About 1856 he moved to Oxford from Lafayette Springs and built the handsome residence now owned by Mrs. Bem Price.[21]

19. *The Observer* (Oxford), April 27, 1844, p. 2.
20. Hathorn, *Lafayette County,* pp. 154-6.
21. "Some Early History of Lafayette County, Mississippi," Compiled by David Reese Chapter D.A.R., Begun in October 1922, Typewritten MS., University of Mississippi Library, unpaged.

Contributing much to the atmosphere of the community was the establishing in Oxford of the Federal Court for the District of Northern Mississippi, which still holds its sessions in the Federal Building. The presence of the federal court in Oxford would mean an influx of lawyers, more than just a county seat would have had in the flush times. Jacob Thompson and L.Q.C. Lamar were typical. As has been said, most of these lawyers moving into a new community would not have been already established, as Thompson was, but would have their fortunes and their reputations yet to make. These men were from the older states of the South, especially the Carolinas and Tennessee. Of course, some succeeded and others failed; but however successful, they established the political and legal orientation of the region. Coming from where they did, they would carry into Mississippi the legal customs of these older Southern states, though modified perhaps by the pioneer environment.

Joseph G. Baldwin's book describes in considerable detail the early courts. Of great importance was the social atmosphere surrounding a court session. Whether federal or county, the session meant a country holiday for the townspeople and the farmers who followed the cases with close attention. What particularly interested the crowd of loungers was extensive and florid oratory. The trial lawyer who was a spellbinder was assured of several days' notoriety after an eloquent speech. These rural observers were delighted when one lawyer outsmarted another. Such games of legal wit became a part of American folklore everywhere on the frontier. To this day one hears such stories told about the legal career of Lincoln in Illinois. But in the stories of Northern law practice there is not so much emphasis upon rhetoric, bombast, and hifalutin oratory. The lawyers in Illinois, for example, frequently devoted their energies to strategy, as in the famous case of Lincoln and the almanac, but in Mississippi the high-sounding phrase was the essential part of the lawyer's equipment. The result of all this rhetoric in the Mississippi country was an unusual emphasis upon the importance of the spoken word. And the exact meaning of a word was less important than its picturesqueness or colorful connotations.

When the Democrats of eastern and northern Mississippi took the political control of the state from the Natchez Whigs, these young lawyers occupied most of the political offices. But what were the intangible forces behind these tangible changes? What were the values of a community such as Oxford after the young lawyers had seemingly won their victory? Were the goals, the values of the average people of Oxford identical with those of the average people of Illinois, for example? Illinois is a good contrast because it became a state in 1819, only two years after Mississippi. If one depends solely upon the evidence of the struggle of Whigs and Democrats, a resemblance between the two states is apparent. Not only are there resemblances, but also there were differences between the Illinois and the Mississippi of the 1840's, almost as many as those of today. To understand the differences, we must turn to intangible values. A quotation from a Vicksburg newspaper of the period expresses a sentiment that must have played an important role in the life of everyone in Oxford.

> A large plantation and negroes are the *Ultima Thule* of every Southern gentleman's ambition. For this the lawyer pores over his dusty tomes, the merchant measures his tape, the doctor rolls

> his pills, the editor drives his quill and the mechanic his plane—all, all who dare aspire at all, look to this as the goal of their ambition. The mind is used, from childhood, to contemplate it, and the first efforts are all lost if the objects in life should be changed. The mind is thus trained from infancy to think of and prepare for the attainment of this end.[22]

Rome conquered Greece politically, but the gods of Greece became the gods of Rome. So it was with Natchez. The goals of Natchez became the goals of Oxford, and Natchez remained until the Civil War the social center for Mississippi. Jackson had the capitol, but Natchez had the dreams. What might be called the Natchez values have prevailed in much of Mississippi and the South until the present. A modified version of these values appears in the novels of Caroline Gordon. With sophisticated and intellectual overtones, they are present in the symposium from Nashville, Tennessee, *I'll Take My Stand,* published in 1930. The values sought are twentieth-century versions of those of early Natchez.

This factor is one of the most important in explaining the present decay of a town such as Oxford. This is not the only factor: for example, soil erosion and depletion make their contributions to the incipient decadence. Perhaps the very conjunction of the barren soil with the Natchez dreams is what makes the tragedy of Oxford so bitterly real. In the contrast between the Natchez dream and the robust values described by Reuben Davis (p. 27) there is dramatic illustration of the change from vigor to genteel decay.

The next important event, after the invasion by

22. Vicksburg *Sun,* April 9, 1860. Quoted in Rainwater, *Mississippi, Storm Center of Secession,* p. 203.

the lawyers and the flush times, was the establishment of the University of Mississippi near Oxford in 1848. Recall that the reason for naming the town Oxford (at the suggestion of Isom) was to secure the location of the state university. A law had been passed by Congress in 1815 on the founding of schools in land sold by the Federal government in the new territories and states. Under this law the proceeds from the sales of one-sixteenth of each township were to be set aside for the support of the common schools, and the land sales from one entire township were mandated for a "seminary of learning."[23] Thus the new state of Mississippi had a sum of money to use for educational purposes. Consciously following the model of Virginia, the state legislature with the township proceeds "started a literary fund in 1821 with the proviso that neither principal nor interest was to be used until it amounted to $50,000. That point was reached in 1833, and the legislature then ordered it to be invested in stock of the Planters' Bank 6f Mississippi."[24] During the Panic of 1837 this bank closed, and there was no more literary fund. The same fate befell most of the funds for the common schools, and consequently, prior to the Civil War, the schools of Mississippi never amounted to much. In 1846 the state passed a law to support public common schools, but it never appropriated much money to back up its good intentions. But finally in 1844 the University of Mississippi was chartered and a board of trustees appointed. They met at various times to get the university organized for its first classes in the fall of 1848.

23. *Historical Catalogue of the University of Mississippi 1846-1907* (Nashville, 1910), p. 1.

24. Charles S. Sydnor, *The Development of Southern Sectionalism, 1819-1848,* Vol. V, *A History of the South* (Baton Rouge, 1948), p. 61.

At a meeting of the board of trustees on July 12, 1848, one discussion well illustrates a changing intellectual attitude in the South. A furious debate took place over the resolution "That the evidences of Christianity be taught in the University." Wilkinson moved to substitute the resolution that the university should have a chaplain (implying that his role would be a non-teaching one) instead of the compulsory course. This amendment was defeated with only two yeas, Wilkinson and Pegues. Then the original motion carried with the same two men voting against it. [25] In protest against this definite establishment of the University of Mississippi on a Christian foundation, one trustee, "a bold, pronounced infidel," resigned. But from that time to the present, no further objection has been registered. The formal teaching of the evidences of Christianity lasted until 1930. [26]

We can better understand the significance of this board's vote if we look at the intellectual atmosphere of Virginia in the late 18th and early 19th centuries. Under the leadership of Thomas Jefferson and others the South was decidedly deistic and liberal in religion. New England, by contrast, during the early part of this period was conservative. The Hartford Wits, before Barlow went to France and got acquainted with Paine, were considered New England's bright and shining literary lights. One of them especially, Timothy Dwight, later President of Yale, saw to it that they stuck to the current party line of Federalism and the dogmas of orthodox Calvinism. But in 1848

25. Florence E. Campbell (ed.), *Journal of the Minutes of the Board of Trustees of University of Mississippi 1845-60*, M.A. Thesis, University of Mississippi Library (1939), pp. 60-1.

26. James A. Cabaniss, *A History of the University of Mississippi* (University, Miss., 1949), p. 196.

Emerson had replaced Dwight in New England, and the Methodist and Baptist circuit riders had replaced Jefferson in the South. Now the South's intellectual atmosphere was conservative and New England's was liberal. Actually, the dispute among these trustees represents one of the last thoroughgoing defeats of the old Jeffersonian spirit. Evidences of Christianity became a part of the required curriculum, since all students until 1870 took the same schedule.

As an interesting sidelight, the diversified teaching program of the first president of the university reveals much about the educational attitudes of the region. He taught classes in mental and moral philosophy, belles lettres, political economy, and international law.[27] The political economy was undoubtedly that of Adam Smith as strained through the minds of the South Carolina writers on the subject. And the Scottish school of common sense realism would probably have held sway in mental and moral philosophy.

The students of the new university were exclusively men although as yet the South had not had much experience with universities for men. The South had usually sent its young men to Northern colleges and universities. There were, actually, more girls' schools than boys' in the South, though most of these girls' schools could hardly be called institutions of higher learning.

During the twenty years before the Civil War, the South started several colleges for boys, so that their minds would not be contaminated by the abolitionists in the North.[28] Because of the date of its founding, the University of Mississippi became part of this general movement. By the

27. *Historical Catalogue*, p. 7.
28. Edward Mayes, *History of Education in Mississippi* (Washington, 1899), p. 126.

early fifties Longstreet, then president of the university, "was a member of a committee appointed at the Charleston Commercial Convention to provide orthodox textbooks for use in Southern schools, for books by Northern writers were considered hostile to Southern institutions." [29] By the fifties the South didn't even want its boys reading books written by Northerners, let alone going to Northern schools. It should be added. as later events proved so tragically, that this kind of censorship builds up a hostility to all new ideas, or to ideas eternally new, and this is very much a part of the ante-bellum Southern attitudes.

One of those subtle ways through which a society reveals itself is in its architecture. In a community such as Oxford, there were few public buildings besides the courthouse already mentioned; so it becomes important to look at the homes of the people. As one would expect in a semi-frontier settlement in the early 19th century in this country, the first houses were built of logs with either dirt or puncheon floors. [30] Soon more permanent dwellings were erected, and in not too many years houses with some aspirations to pretentiousness were being built. Five brick and stone homes were built between 1840 and 1850; in the same period 469 wooden houses. [31] This region was, as it is today, covered by trees, with not much stone available except when brought in from a distance. And brick was mostly made on the grounds of the house by the slaves. Even for the wooden houses brick was used for the formal front walk, for the foundations, for the chimneys,

29. Charles S. Sydnor, *Slavery in Mississippi* (New York, 1939), pp. 244-5.
30. "Some Early History of Lafayette County," unpaged.
31. Hathorn, *Lafayette County,* p. 98.

and for some of the slave quarters. Much of this original brick is still to be found in Oxford.

Among the first built of what I have called the pretentious houses, there remain in Oxford today three with identical designs (a fourth seemingly is a replica of the same front elevation), which were apparently built at nearly the same time. The two I am able to date were constructed in 1848 and 1850. Of interest is that one of the four is now owned by William Faulkner. All of them are white, wooden, two-story dwellings. Each has a brick walk up to the front entrance, though the front lawns are landscaped differently. Above the entrance is a balcony with a second-story door leading onto it. There is a formal Greek portico on the front of each house with four, square wooden columns extending for two stories up to the triangular pediment. The first reaction of a visitor to these houses (there is a similar one in Como, twenty-six or twenty-seven miles northwest of Oxford, and a few others scattered about the countryside) is that these are the work of a professional architect who spent several years in the locality. Closer examination inside the houses, especially the blending of the interior design with that of the exterior, leads one to the probable conclusion that these were built by a local builder, without professional architectural training, working from drawings in some pattern book, of which there were many published both in England and America at that time. Whoever this builder was, he learned how to build this type of house, the people of the region liked it, and he continued to build what he knew. Also, it should be added, these houses are obviously built by a good carpenter. The four in Oxford are, to use the names of the owners (summer, 1949): the Faulkner, Culley, Tate, and Chandler homes. The questions of who the builder was and what pattern book was used, I cannot answer. Half a dozen names have been suggested to me, but no one person seems to have the conclusive proof.

Professional architects did work in Oxford at different times before the Civil War. William Nichols was the architect for the University's Lyceum building, whose cornerstone was laid July 14, 1856.[32] The presence of another architect is shown by the following advertisement from an Oxford newspaper:

> M.J. McGuire, Architect & Civil Engineer, Oxford, Miss., Respectfully tenders his services to the public in the above branches. He will promptly attend to drawing plans for all manner of Buildings, in the various styles of Architecture; the construction of bridges—draw Specifications and Contracts between parties; superintend the measurement of all work in the Building line, also, excavations.[33]

Oxford must have been a rather active, growing community for a professional architect to set up practice, even if he was a jack of all trades.

Another architect temporarily present in the community was Richard Upjohn. He designed St. Peter's Episcopal Church of Oxford, which was built in 1858 and '59. Upjohn is better known as the architect of Trinity Church in New York City, finished in 1846. F. A. P. Barnard, President of Columbia University from 1864 to 1889, was rector of St. Peter's from 1855 to 1861 and at that time he was also either president or chancellor of the University of Mississippi. Apparently it was his influence that brought Upjohn from

32. Cabaniss, *A History of the University of Mississippi*, pp. 7-8.
33. *The Democratic Flag* (Oxford), May 19, 1852, p. 4.

New York City to design the church at Oxford.[34]

The story of the Pegues house on North Lamar Street is an interesting one. A. H. Pegues was on the board of trustees of the university and started to build the most pretentious house in the town in 1859. The set of drawings made for the house are signed "C. Vaux, architect, N. Y. 1859," with some of the detailed drawings dated 1860. (An interesting note for Faulkner readers, local tradition in Oxford has it that the architect for the house was "a fellow with a French name.") Calvert Vaux was a New York architect of the firm of Olmsted and Vaux, who as landscape architects designed Prospect Park, Brooklyn; Central Park, New York City; South Park, Chicago; and other well-known parks and estates. Olmsted is perhaps better known as the author of *The Cotton Kingdom* and other writings describing his travels through the South before the Civil War. That Vaux ever visited Oxford is doubtful, there being nothing in the drawings to indicate any on-the-spot work. The Pegues house was not finished by the time the war broke out in 1861 and remained unfinished until after the war, when a new owner finished the place as simply as he could (deviations from the original plans are noted in pencil on the drawings) and named the place Ammadelle after his wife. Ammadelle is apparently the only brick ante-bellum house in the town now standing.

Transportation, like architecture, adapted itself to the needs of the community. The steamboats going up the Tallahatchie as far as Wyatt have already been mentioned. Something of the extent

34. Information about the church obtained from a scrapbook kept by Mrs. Edward McCrady, now in the Mary Buie Museum Oxford, Miss.

and difficulties of such transportation, with its resultant connection with New Orleans, is revealed by the following advertisement:

> Vicksburg, Jan. 20, 1844. The steamer Lucy Long. Broady, Master. This new and substantial Steamer will leave the above named place the 28th of January, 1844. This 400 hole [*sic*] boat will run as a Regular Packet, from Vicksburg to the Rocky-Ford, on the Tallahachie; and make trips on the Yockinapatapha, as far as California during the season. Lucy Long has now nearly got her engine completed and will be [in] superior order. This *light draught* Boat will ply as a regular packet from the mouth of Cold Water, in low water to the mouth of Tippali, and act in concert with a good, safe boat to reship Cotton, and as she is determined to be a Regular Packet in *that trade,* she hopes to receive a liberal share of patronage.[35]

Changes in transportation explain certain changes in Oxford's relations to larger towns of the South. The early steamboats tied Oxford economically and socially to Vicksburg, Natchez, and ultimately New Orleans. The later development of land transportation made Memphis assume the importance for Oxford that the cities on the southern Mississippi once had. Today the people of Oxford go to Memphis to speculate on cotton, to buy clothes and liquor, to see shows, and to spend their week-ends. In the 1830's and '40's they probably took a steamboat down the river when they went on such excursions.

The earliest attempts at organized transportation overland were stage coaches to Memphis and to other towns. During the '40's and '50's the rivers and streams were mostly without bridges, and the stage coaches had to depend upon ferries.

The story of the railroads goes back to 1837,

35. *The Observer* (Oxford), February 10, 1844, p. 3.

when the Pontotoc, Oxford and Delta R. R. was incorporated. The panic of that year promptly put an end to the scheme.[36] The Mississippi Central, now the Illinois Central Railroad, reached Oxford about 1857. Something of the vitality of the community is to be seen in a story connected with the building of this railroad. University is a separate incorporated town adjoining Oxford to the west. Between the two towns run the railroad tracks. Here the leaders of Oxford and the university had their slaves, especially those of T. D. Isom, dig a very deep cut for the tracks. Legend has it that this cut was made so that passengers could see the new buildings on the new campus. Unfortunately the energetic workers cut it so deep that all the passengers could see was red clay banks. Today this cut is still the deepest on the Illinois Central.[37]

A few words should be said about the early newspapers of Oxford.[38] A good many copies of these are on file in the State Archives in Jackson. An examination of them shows that, as elsewhere in this country, the newspapers reflected the political ideas of the editor and were organs of opinion not of news. None of these papers, all weeklies, survived for long. Like the average country paper of today, Oxford's were full of clippings from the

36. Hathorn, *Lafayette County,* p. 124.
37. Federal Writers' Project, *Mississippi,* p. 259.
38. After 1850 the book advertisements from Northern publishers (see p. 32) were fewer and fewer and disappeared altogether by the late 1850's. Of incidental interest to the reader of Walt Whitman is the following advertisement:

> Franklin Evans, or the Inebriate a tale of the times, by a popular American author. Terms.— It is issued in an Extra New World, (octavo) at 12 1/2 cents single; ten copies for 1 dollar or 2 dollars for hundred. Let the orders be early. Address postpaid, J. Winchester, 30 Ann Street, New York.

The Observer (Oxford), August 19, 1843, p. 3.

exchanges. In *The Observer* for October 14, 1843, the story by J. J. Hooper, "Taking the Census," is printed in its entirety without any mention of either author or source.

During most of the period there were both Whig and Democratic papers. A result of the 1850 Compromise and its political aftermath in Mississippi was the establishment in Oxford of a newspaper called *The Constitution,* which represented the extremist Southern point of view. Its first issue, March 22, 1851, carried as a motto, "Equality in the Union, or independence out of it." The paper lasted only a little over six months, it not being coincidental that the Whigs, who favored the Compromise, won the elections of that year.

The general atmosphere of Oxford just before the Civil War was vital and vigorous. Its leaders were really leaders. Jacob Thompson was Secretary of the Interior in Buchanan's cabinet. Lucius Quintus Cincinnatus Lamar, later to secure fame in Washington, was practicing law and teaching at the university. A. B. Longstreet was president of the university from 1849 to 1856, and he was well known throughout the South. His book, *Georgia Scenes,* is still read. F. A. P. Barnard, who became president of the university in 1856, was a person of considerable intellectual vigor and later became prominent at Columbia University. R. A. Hill was already famous as a judge of the district federal court. The general picture has been described:

> The institution [University of Mississippi] drew some of the South's most brilliant minds to Oxford, and until the outbreak of the War between the States, a society of culture and gaiety flourished. An opera house was built, bringing many famous entertainers to the town. Young men held tilting tournaments that resem-

> bled in their color and pageantry the jousts of Scott's romances. Sober-minded scholars divided their attention between their books and addresses to the crowds gathered on the courthouse square.[39]

Though the imitation of Scott's romances appears to our hindsight as an indication of potential decay, we can hardly ignore the general vitality. Oxford was alive in a way that no local Babbitt need be ashamed of. Unfortunately the 1860 census does not give the population of the town, but by a process of deduction from the 1870 figures and the incomplete returns for 1850, a probable population of about 1,500 is arrived at. I frankly doubt that many American towns of 1,500 could then surpass the vigor of this community.

However, looking closely at this vigor, we can perceive its incompleteness. A show of intellectuality was more important than intellectuality itself. In spite of the abilities of certain individuals, the town as a whole seems, in retrospect, to have been wanting in the higher qualities of moral and intellectual stamina. It is as though the vigor of the community was only at the level of physical courage, and this is true for the South as a whole at this time. High-sounding words by resounding orators were the answers to crises. When words didn't answer and war finally broke out, the glory of the military (physical courage) was extolled, idealized, and sentimentalized. Something of this glorification of the role of the soldier (and the politician) still remains in the South.

Again in retrospect, one of the moral failures of the pre-Civil War Oxford was the institution of slavery. As a newly settled area in the South

39. Federal Writers' Project, *Mississippi,* p. 255.

it needed slaves and developed a sentiment in favor of slavery as an institution:

> It was the relative pressure of labor costs that determined the current attitude toward slavery. Sentiment for slavery rose with the accession of new groups of planters to the land and fell as the new landowners improved their economic status. In the 1820's, when the cotton land around Natchez was well taken up and the planter had accumulated means to hire labor, there began a strong movement to return the slaves to Africa. But in 1830 and 1832, when new cotton lands [including Lafayette county] were opened and people moved in with the debts of their first few years of operation impending, the feeling for African colonization waned.[40]

In spite of slavery's being accepted and believed in, it should be remembered that most of Lafayette county is hill country. This being true, the proportion of Negroes in the population has always been smaller in that county than in the state. In 1840 only 44% of the population were Negro slaves. In 1850 it was 40.6%. In 1860 it was again approximately 44%. Of the total white population in 1860 less than 7% (606 out of 8,989) owned any slaves.[41] This was the population which so enthusiastically went to war in 1861.

I have dwelt overlong on this story of the rise of Oxford because Oxford in the 1850's was at its peak of vitality. Its story from then on is one of slowly decreasing vigor. That the Civil War destroyed Oxford is not true. The seeds of decay were already present in the 1850's, as I have tried to show. The war no doubt hastened tremendously the decaying process, but one of its chief effects was to provide an excuse for lowered morale

40. *Ibid.,* p. 98.
41. Hathorn, *Lafayette County,* p. 86.

and ineffective leadership. In many ways the Civil War still provides a well-nigh universal rationalization for failures, no matter how picayune.[42]

At the State Secession Convention on January 7, 1861, Lafayette county had two representatives: L. Q. C. Lamar and Dr. T. D. Isom. Lamar was a leader of the secessionists and presented the final ordinance of secession on the floor of the convention on January 9th. Dr. Isom, an old-time Whig and Oxford's leading physician during nearly all of the town's 19th century history, opposed secession vigorously.[43] After the ordinance had passed, he signed it and threw in his lot with the majority. Thus it can be seen that sentiment for secession was by no means unanimous in the county. An incident at the university also illustrates this division of opinion. Immediately after the passing of the ordinance of secession, a Mississippi flag was raised over one dormitory. Over a neighboring dormitory, a U. S. flag was raised and kept there for ten days.[44] Nor were the faculty any more united than the students. Barnard left for the North in the fall of 1861. The professor of chemistry, Edward C. Boynton, had earlier been dismissed from the faculty for his

42. After I had written these sentences, I found confirmation of them in a statement by Jonathan Daniels, speaking as a Southerner: "For all its tragedy and loss, the South was never so deeply stricken as it believed it was. [The legend of the war] became the somnabulent alibi for every fault of the section and for every deficiency of its people." Quoted in Ernest E. Leisy, *The American Historical Novel* (Norman, Okla., 1950), p. 190.

43. An interesting footnote to the career of Dr. Isom: "The large magnolia tree in the Isom yard was brought by his bride, Sarah McGeehee, from South Carolina in a cigar box." Holt, *Oxford, Mississippi,* p. 14. Faulkner uses a modification of this story in *Sartoris.*

44. Mayes, *Education in Mississippi,* p. 152.

Union sentiments and finally became an officer in the Union Army.[45]

At the university some of the students in the spring of 1861 organized themselves into a company called the University Greys and soon left the campus. For the fall term so few students showed up that the school was closed for the duration of the war.

The first tangible experience of the war for the town occurred just after the battle of Shiloh on June 6-7, 1862. Many of the Confederate wounded from that battle were sent to Oxford and placed in the vacant buildings of the university. They remained there until November of that year, when they were sent to Grenada, because of the impending approach of Grant and his army. Grant spent most of December in Oxford, apparently using the town as a temporary headquarters. No noteworthy incidents were recorded of that occupation. After Grant left, the Confederate General Forrest used the town as his headquarters and the university buildings again as a hospital. And for the rest of the war these buildings were put to this use.[46] Primarily, therefore, the town was part of the home-front and saw service as a hospital center.

One exception occurred on August 9, 1864. On that day General A. J. Smith on a foray from Tennessee burned all but one of Oxford's business establishments on the town square.[47] The center of the town was almost completely destroyed, and at the southeast outskirts, Jacob Thompson's house was burned, probably because Thompson at the

45. Cabaniss, *A History of the University of Mississippi,* pp. 44 and 57-8.

46. Jemmy C. Johnson, "The Civil War Hospital at the University," *Publ. Miss. Hist. Soc.,* XII, pp. 94-106.

47. Medford Evans, "Oxford, Mississippi," *Southwest Review,* XV (October, 1929), p. 50.

time was known to be in Canada trying to secure the assistance of Canadians for the Confederacy. The university was not touched. Two or three factors may explain this. One was undoubtedly the reputation of Barnard in the North, since in 1864 he had become president of Columbia University. Another was the early friendship between Dr. A. J. Quinche and Grant. Quinche was caretaker of the buildings during the war and had taught in Illinois before coming to Mississippi. And of course the school was a couple of miles from the center of the town and may have been in use as a hospital at the time. It is interesting that folklore in the community has run together these expeditions of Grant in 1862 and Smith in 1864, and today one hears in the county frequent allusion to the time "Grant burned Oxford."

In the area surrounding the town there was much guerrilla warfare. Both armies, at various times, were concerned over the theft of horses. It was probably to maintain, as much as possible, local law and order that groups of irregular cavalry operated in the region under the general command of Forrest. Colonel William C. Falkner, the great-grandfather of the present novelist, led one such irregular regiment which operated around Oxford.

But in spite of the wounded in the hospital, the burning of the town, and guerrilla activity, the war came to its end in April, 1865. Actually after General Smith's raid the theater of war moved to the east and must have seemed rather remote during those last six or eight months. The "cause" was lost for Oxford much before Appomattox. Something of the breakdown in morale during those last few months, a pattern quite general in the South, can be perceived in the words of a contemporary Southern historian:

> Why did the Confederacy fail? The forces leading to defeat were many but they may be summed up in this one fact: The people did not will hard enough and long enough to win. Wars in those times were not inevitably won by the side strongest in material resources and numbers of soldiers; otherwise the South would have been foolhardy to enter the struggle. It was not the last dollar or the last soldier but the last ounce of will power or morale. In this realm the Confederacy started out with boundless enthusiasm which began sadly to deteriorate as early as 1862. ... As important as were the blockades and the Federal navy, the breakdown of transportation, short-term enlistments and the election of officers by the soldiers, the failure to send cotton to Europe during the first part of the war, and other forces, the fact remains that the Confederacy never fully utilized the human and material resources it had. It never succeeded in developing an *esprit de corps,* either in its civil or military organization, and in that sense it did not deserve to win.[48]

Classes were resumed at the university in September 1865, and the town reverted to peace-time occupations with Reconstruction hanging over its head. It is pointless here to give too many details of Reconstruction in the community, since the pattern of life was quite similar to that in other towns of the deep South.[49] The Ku Klux Klan (local legend has it that General Forrest came to Oxford to organize the Oxford group) and other semi-military organizations were active. One white woman was killed by a band of Negroes, and at various times about fifty Negroes were killed. A few details should suffice to illustrate certain attitudes prevalent at the time.

48. E. Merton Coulter, *The Confederate States of America, 1861-65* (Baton Rouge, 1950), pp. 566-7.
49. For a complete, though unscientific, account of this period see Julia Kendel, "Reconstruction in Lafayette County," *Publ. Miss. Hist. Soc.,* XIII, pp. 223-71.

On October 2nd and 3rd, 1867, the Scott-like tournaments, held in Oxford during the 1850's, were revived "for the benefit of the Oxford Graveyard." [50] This event shows the desire and probably even the expectation of the citizens of Oxford to return to "normalcy" — to act as though the events of the war had not happened. This attitude is a common one after all wars and can easily be remembered as the pattern after World War II. But normalcy was not for Oxford, and soon the Freedman's Bureau and the physical hardships of Reconstruction were on the town.

But the people of Oxford adjusted themselves to the situation as best they could. Miss Kendel, a citizen of the town, writing in 1900 when many of the participants in and prejudices of the Reconstruction were still alive, recorded in a spirit of revealing candor: "The freedman's bureau was rather beneficial to the whites in the control of labor. The agent of the bureau could easily be won over on the side of the white man by the use of a little money." [51] In other words, apparently Reconstruction wasn't as hard on Oxford as Oxford today would have us believe. Soldiers occupied the town from 1868 to 1875, but life went along just about as it had. Oxford citizens must have found means of placating various Reconstruction officials that some towns either wouldn't or couldn't use. The capable leaders of the town from before the Civil War were almost all still alive. Barnard was at Columbia and Thompson was in Europe, but Lamar, Hill, and others were still around and active.

To the university and to the public schools in general, Reconstruction was kind. The authorities did not interfere with the operations of the univer-

50. *Oxford Eagle,* December 10, 1936, p. 23.
51. Kendel, "Reconstruction in Lafayette County," p. 254.

sity, except in 1870 when the state legislature reorganized the board of trustees.[52] The new trustees made some changes in the basic curriculum, introducing history courses for the first time.[53] In the same year curricula leading to the degrees of B.S., B.Ph., and C.E. were added to the original B.A. program.[54] These changes are all in the direction of what we today call democratization of the college program. Something of the same democratization and increase in educational opportunities took place in the secondary schools of the state at about the same time. The changes made at the university and in the public schools were permanently influential and much of the pattern of the education in Mississippi therefore stems from the activities of the Reconstruction officials. As a matter of fact, it can probably be said that education was one of the few positive contributions to the state by the Reconstruction.

But let us return to the town of Oxford itself and take another over-all view of it. Before the Civil War there was a tremendous vitality in the community. Has the Civil War destroyed that vitality? The answer to that question would have to be no. The vitality is not what it once was, but it is still there. At the same time it must be admitted that there are differences between the pre- and post-Civil War patterns. One noticeable thing is that the leaders both before and after the war are the same people; but they're all that much older, and they're fewer in number. Barnard remained at Columbia. When Thompson came back from Europe, he moved to Memphis. But most of the rest are active in Oxford. In 1872, when the Reconstruction in the state had three

52. Mayes, *Education in Mississippi,* pp. 162-3.
53. *Historical Catalogue,* p. 49.
54. *Ibid.,* p. 12.

years to go, Lamar was elected to Congress as the only Democratic representative from the state. Two years later he gave in Congress his famous eulogy on Sumner after the latter's death. In 1885 he went into Cleveland's cabinet as Secretary of the Interior. From 1887 to his death he was a member of the United States Supreme Court.[55] But men like Lamar were not being replaced by younger men. There were no young men to lead after the Lamars and the Hills had either died or moved away. Oxford had produced one generation of great men and could not do it again. The period from 1865 to 1890 may well be thought of as the Indian summer of Oxford. The town was starting to live in the past, not for the future.[56]

Two developments which are part of the story of the decay of Oxford can not easily be dated. Both took place gradually. The first of these is the slow deterioration of the soil. The Mississippi River flows all along the western border of the state. This river and those flowing directly into the Gulf of Mexico drain Mississippi. Without the disturbing hand of profit-seeking man the land of the state would be little affected by this drainage except by occasional overflows of the rivers in springtime. But profit-seeking man has been all over the state of Mississippi. The principal crop of the state since 1800 has been and still is — cotton. Cotton, like corn, robs the soil of nitrogen and of various minerals. Also, the successful growth of almost any farm crop

55. Evans, "Oxford, Mississippi," p. 53.

56. Of interest to those who saw the movie version of *Intruder in the Dust* is the information that the present courthouse and jail in Oxford were built in 1871. The courthouse used the foundations of the pre-Civil War building, but the rest of it was all constructed anew. The architecture of the building resembles the old one, as a look at a picture of the old building, found in the Mary Buie Museum, will reveal.

demands that all plant growth other than the crop-producing plant be removed. Cotton left to itself will not hold the soil in place during floods or even during an afternoon shower. As a result we have two changes taking place simultaneously — soil depletion and soil erosion. A depleted soil will erode more easily than one not depleted, so the two developments are somewhat interdependent. In this soil depletion and erosion the South resembles Spain, which has been going through this process since the 17th century; in fact, in many ways the cultural decay of the two regions has striking resemblances for the historian to ponder over. Even the rich Delta country of northwestern Mississippi suffers from soil depletion though not from erosion. Soil changes are not the kind of thing that one can measure meaningfully with any kind of yardstick, but the evidence of the change is visible from a cursory examination.

The second development can be dated roughly; yet I find that what I am saying is a matter of inference, not evidence. Even though I must infer, I do not hesitate to say that the industrialization of the South along with the soil destruction in Lafayette county is more important in the history of Oxford than the Civil War and Reconstruction. Though W. J. Cash in his book, *The Mind of the South,* shows how the cotton mill in the South followed the paternalism of the plantation system, what is important for Oxford is that Oxford developed no mills, no factories, nor any other industries. In the 1870's and the 1880's Birmingham, Alabama, got its steel industry running at full blast. What would you do if you were an ambitious young man in Oxford in the '70's and '80's? Those with vigor were drained off by the steel mills of Birmingham, the docks of Mobile and New Orleans, and whatever Memphis had to offer. Emigration by the more independent-minded people — whites and blacks alike — began at this time and has ever since characterized Oxford and so many other communities in the deep South. Children keep being born in Oxford — more so proportionately than in a similar Northern town — but successful hatcheries do not necessarily produce successful cultural patterns.

It may be a bit of an interruption to the story of Oxford to stop here and talk about Colonel W. C. Falkner, but Colonel Falkner does provide some of the historical material from which his great-grandson, the novelist, draws. Also, Falkner is typical of those leaders of the Confederacy who were active after the war.[57] Of Welsh descent he was born in Knox County, Tennessee, July 6, 1826. Shortly after his birth the family moved to Missouri, where his father died, and then the family returned to Tennessee. At the age of seventeen Falkner walked to Ripley, Mississippi, where he had relatives. Here, after many difficulties, he became a lawyer and a successful planter. He served in the Mexican War. During the 1850's his political affiliations were those of an old-line Whig also interested in the Know-Nothing party. At the outbreak of the Civil War he organized and outfitted a company and was elected Colonel of the 2nd Mississippi Regiment. In April, 1862, he was defeated for re-election as Colonel by John W. Stone, later governor of Mississippi, and returned to Ripley from Virginia. Then he had the command of the irregular regiment of cavalry already mentioned. After the

57. See Alexander L. Bondurant, "William C. Falkner Novelist," *Publ. Miss. Hist. Soc., III* (1900), pp. 113-27. When the contemporary novelist's first book, *The Marble Faun,* was published, a misprint made *Falkner* into *Faulkner,* and so it has remained.

war Falkner resumed his law practice in Ripley and became active in the Democratic party. He organized the Ripley Railroad, now part of the Gulf, Mobile and Southern, which was finished in 1872. During the 1880's he wrote several novels, the most popular of which was *The White Rose of Memphis,* 1882.

> Colonel Falkner fought many duels, and it is a family legend that when he made a bitter enemy of his old friend and railroad associate Col. R. J. Thurmond, by defeating him for the State Legislature in 1899 [1889], he refused to arm himself, saying that he already had killed too many men and did not want to kill any more. On the day of Falkner's second election to the legislature [Nov. 5, 1889] Thurmond shot him dead on the main street of Ripley.[58]

The turbulent post-war career of Colonel Falkner is paralleled by Oxford's unsettled life between 1875, the ending of the Reconstruction, and 1900. Crime, the frequent aftermath of war, was prevalent. An apparently unsuccessful attempt to curb this crime was the introduction of prohibition for Lafayette county in 1882. The result was the appearance of "blind tigers" and other bootlegging activities.[59]

Yellow fever was a constant threat during these years in towns such as Oxford. It is true that the epidemic of 1878 which created so much havoc in Memphis skipped by the county, though the entire county was quarantined and all business suspended for two months.[60] Later, in 1898,

58. Federal Writers' Project, *Mississippi,* p. 458.
59. WPA Manuscript Records Lafayette County, State Archives, Jackson, Mississippi.
60. Letter from M. D. Vance, *Report of the Mississippi State Board of Health for the Years 1878-79* (Jackson, 1879), p. 111.

Oxford had a small yellow fever epidemic. For two months, September and October, the town was evacuated and disinfected. In November the populace returned and the schools and the university reopened on November 15th. Twelve deaths were recorded.[61] Since then there have been no major outbreaks of disease except for the influenza epidemic following World War I.

The story of the people of Oxford and the town itself becomes rather colorless and dead. Much of the reason for this lack of color is the apathy of the inhabitants and their leaders. To see the pattern of events as a whole, we should look at the state of Mississippi at the turn of the century. In the 1890's the state had been affected by the Populist revolt, though not nearly as much as had the Midwest or certain other parts of the South, particularly where Tom Watson's influence was strong. The primary (all-white) had just been taken out of the convention and made a matter of election. In 1904 James K. Vardaman was placed in office as governor. His election symbolized the coming of political power to the "red-necks." During the latter part of the 19th century most of the members of the state legislature had been ex-Confederate officers. They had held leadership before; so the people retained them. Now Vardaman appealed directly to the red-necks (so called from their working in the sun all day), and they put him into office. Racial supremacy and segregation were openly used as a means of acquiring political office. In 1904 the state "Jim Crow" law was passed. We are now in the era of the political demagogue, perhaps best sym-

61. *Report of the Mississippi State Board of Health from September 30, 1897 to September 30, 1899* (Jacksonville, Florida, 1900), pp. 81-3. This report states that Oxford is "comparatively free from malaria," p. 81.

bolized in the mind of the average person by Bilbo, one of Vardaman's followers. An Oxford lawyer, Lee M. Russell, of the law firm of Falkner and Russell, was lieutenant-governor of the state during Bilbo's first term as governor, 1916-1920. Russell himself was governor from 1920 to 1924. Political power through the votes of the red-necks is common to most of the deep South since 1900 — for example, Talmadge and the wool-hat boys in Georgia, Long and the Cajuns in Louisiana, and Pa and Ma Ferguson in Texas.

Today the representatives of the Delta are the dominant political power in Mississippi. But they are not the Delta planter-aristocracy so well portrayed in William Alexander Percy's *Lanterns on the Levee;* rather they are from the corporations controlling large stretches of fertile Delta valley. This political control is more evident in the state legislature than anywhere else. The present governor of the state — Fielding L. Wright — comes from the Delta. Many of the political struggles in the state are to be explained by the clash of interests between the people of the Delta and those on the hills behind (such as in Oxford) who are jealous of the valley prosperity and of the large percentage of Negroes there.

A phenomenon less obvious than this yet equally influential is what became known in the 1920's by the term Bible Belt. Its existence was dramatized in 1926 by the Scopes trial in Dayton, Tennessee. It is revealing to find that Mississippi in 1926 placed a law similar to Tennessee's on its statute books.

The story of agriculture in the county until quite recently is a monotonous one. The price of cotton has been one of the chief worries of the average farmer for more than a hundred years. During most of that time the same crops have been planted without too much variation. As cotton production figures reveal, the variation in the crop produced is greater from year to year than it is from century to century. In 1849 production was 10,387 bales; in 1859, 19,282 bales.[62] In 1939 production was 6,975 bales; in 1944, 16,433.[63] Though Lafayette county has always had more acres planted in corn than in cotton, emotionally cotton is still the most important crop for the farmers as talking with them will reveal. Something of the difficulties involved in crop growing in the county is indicated by the comment made to me by the local county agent (in 1949). He mentioned that he had been working on a five-acre cotton production improvement program, but that frequently farmers do not have five acres together of tillable land. Today the most important thing happening on the farms of the county is the increased diversification to livestock and leguminous crops instead of the old standbys for this country — cotton and corn. The decrease in the acres planted in cotton between 1909 and 1944, from 38,254 to 22,126 attests to this development.

Since 1933 the various soil conservation programs of the Federal government and state extension services have done much for Lafayette county. There are still large erosion gullies in the county, but they are not nearly as large or as numerous as they were twenty years ago. To one like myself, who has grown up on the black dirt of Iowa, it is amazing to see how this red dirt of Mississippi recovers itself and becomes productive anew. Nature was not unkind to Lafayette county. Now

62. Hathorn, *Lafayette County,* pp. 97-9.
63. From data prepared by the Extension Economics Division, State College, Mississippi. All agricultural figures since 1900 are from this source.

vines have been planted along the gullies and small dams have been built — all to keep the soil from running down into the Mississippi River. Man must fight man to retain what nature has supplied.

Between 1936 and 1940 the Federal government built, about seventeen or eighteen miles northwest of Oxford, the Sardis Dam on the Tallahatchie River as part of its flood control program for the Mississippi River. Behind the dam — a huge (second largest earthwork dam in the world), three-mile-long structure — is contained a large reservoir of water, varying in size depending upon the rainfall or the season of the year. Most of this Sardis Reservoir is in Lafayette county and provides extensive fishing and boating. At its maximum size the water covers about ninety square miles. So important a sport is fishing that during the season one can walk the streets of Oxford after eight o'clock and wonder why everybody is off the streets and apparently home in bed. The answer is that a good many people are home in bed; so that they can be at the reservoir at four in the morning, get in the morning's catch, and be back in Oxford to open up the stores by seven or eight in the morning. Many farms in Lafayette county were flooded by the waters of the reservoir and there is still some local bitterness towards "Delta politics" for the loss of farm land.

Oxford has recently experienced a cultural renascence. Chief among the persons responsible for this is, of course, William Faulkner. But there are others. One is John Faulkner, younger brother of William. John, who also lives in Oxford, has published three novels, two of which — *Dollar Cotton* and *Men Working* — are realistic and rather well written studies of depression conditions. A third novel *Chooky*, recently published, is the story of a child. Stark Young, born in Como, a little over twenty miles west of Oxford, attended and then taught for a while at the University of Mississippi. Having relatives in Oxford, he has frequently visited there and is regarded by many Oxfordians (should one say Oxonians?) as part of the local scene. And he has made use of local materials in his writings. Another person who has made his cultural contributions to the community is John McCrady, who grew up in Oxford. He is a painter, one of whose best known works is "Town Square," which shows a scene in front of the Lafayette county courthouse before its bricks got their coat of white paint. Though not living in Oxford today, McCrady has used the locale of this community frequently in his pictures.

The twentieth century is found in Oxford in different places. In 1938 the town built, with WPA assistance, a city hall. The exterior is an angular, garishly modern structure. The interior of the building is a contrasting taciturn Victorian. It is unfortunate that such a design was chosen, since it clashes with the rest of the community and is merely different, not individual in its quality.

In 1946 the carpenters' union (A. F. L.) organized a local in Oxford and thereby inserted another symbol of the twentieth century. The carpenters' union, always a conservative organization, actually only uses Oxford as a headquarters for a local serving several counties in northwest Mississippi. As a factor in the community the union is negligible as yet. In the summer of 1949 the local had about eighty members, and these were from several counties.

Another intrusion of the twentieth century into Oxford, though also segregated away a bit, is the airport some seven and a half miles south of the town on the Yocona River. Probably this was the nearest stretch of land with enough flat surface that could be found. It is sometimes called Dean Falkner Airport in honor of a brother of the novelist, who was killed in an airplane accident several years ago.

Walking through the streets of Oxford today, one perceives a heavy shadow of the past hanging over those who live in the present. The past with each new generation is becoming increasingly vague, but neither the vividness of the present nor the potentiality of the future has replaced this dependence upon the past. Those in their teens and early twenties seem left high and dry with nothing to cling to either in the past or the present; yet there is something about the community that makes many want to stick to it. Unfortunately, most of those who remain in the community are the ones with the least education and the most family responsibilities. This exodus from the community and even from the state by the better class of young people is more common among the Negroes than it is among the whites, though it is noticeable with both. Those who want to think of the present and hope for the future seem to leave Oxford.

The relations between the white and the Negro are not being helped by having the more intelligent of both races leave the community. The old family servant, such as Dilsey in *The Sound and the Fury,* is becoming a memory. Today the Negroes of Oxford who do domestic service, and there are many, prefer to live in their own houses instead of in quarters supplied either in the main house or in buildings behind the main house. It can be readily understood why the Negroes want to do this, but there is one bad result. In living in their own homes in a place such as Oxford, the Negroes are inevitably shunted off to a district of their own. Formerly the children of the white master and those of the Negro slave-servant played together. Now they no longer do. The gulf between the races is momentarily increasing instead of decreasing, and it becomes more difficult each year to work out satisfactory compromises between the two races, each with its sets of prejudices against the other.

A more hopeful sign in the community is the presence of one of the best country newspapers in Mississippi, *The Oxford Eagle*. And no doubt influenced by the many members of the university faculty in the town, the bookstore operated in conjunction with the newspaper, though small, has a stock of books of a quality that would be envied by most metropolitan stores. The lending-library type of fiction is either just not there or is placed inconspicuously in the background.

The dependence of the community upon Memphis is noticeable. Today no passenger trains pass through Oxford, only local freight trains, but a surfaced highway leads up to Memphis some seventy miles away. As a result the lobby of the Peabody Hotel in Memphis is well known to most of Oxford's white citizens. The ease of getting back and forth to Memphis has almost destroyed bootlegging as a business of any size. (Mississippi is legally dry and Tennessee is not.) In many ways the cultural capital of northern Mississippi is Memphis; just as New Orleans is that of the southern part of the state.

It is interesting to observe the attitude of the people of the community towards the *nouveau riche* — locally defined as one who obtained his family's money after the start of the Civil War. The line of demarcation is very sharp and complete. If money was made in 1860, no matter how, the descendants are "old family." But if money was made in 1865, again no matter how, the family is looked down upon.

Perhaps a suggestive way to end this historical sketch is with some notes I wrote in the summer of 1949 of a visit I made to a small rural community, much like Frenchman's Bend, not far from Oxford. It's about as desolate a place as one could find. One or two hundred inhabitants, mostly Negro. Along the highway there's a string of filling stations and small stores. I noticed that one of the filling stations was opened to wait on a customer and then the attendant locked up the station to go fishing. On a porch of one of the stores a half dozen men were engaged in a vigorous game of dominoes. And they weren't old men either. Most of the players were in their twenties or thirties and made one think of the younger members of the Snopes tribe. A block away from the highway there's a row of deserted houses and store buildings. In a corner one, as dilapidated and unpainted as the rest, a general store still holds forth. I arrived in the town a little before one o'clock and saw the door padlocked like the rest of the row. I assumed the store to be vacant and wondered why one of the natives clumsily hitched himself up the steps to the gallery (covered with a sheet iron awning) and then sat there. In a few minutes the storekeeper came up and unlocked the door and set up business. Three or four people followed him in and almost immediately came out and sat on the gallery for the afternoon's session. A freight train stopped about a hundred yards from the store long enough to drop off the daily mail and express and then lumbered on. On a porch in the block between the old store and the highway I noticed several

Negro women and their children perched on chairs. A white woman drove up and parked and then hollered for one of the children to come over and help her carry something into the store. One of the sitting women relayed the request to the children in general, and gradually one young girl oozed her way over to the car to carry a brief-case into the store. As I walked around, I saw that one of the garage-filling stations had several cars junked in its backyard and along the sides. Of course, the day was hot, but the atmosphere of being punch drunk from the mere act of having to exist is, I suspect, a permanent feature of the place.

III

LEGEND

In moving from the world of Oxford and Lafayette county to the world of Jefferson and Yoknapatawpha county, I want to make clear at once that the two worlds are not the same. Also — and here's the rub — the history found in this chapter is only implied in Faulkner's books. As a word of caution both to the reader and to myself — the kind of history I am writing here, if history be the right word for it, is not the same history found in the usual book by the practising historian. His sources, and mine for the preceding chapter, are the conventional ones — newspapers, scrap-books, visit to the physical scene, talks with different people in Oxford, the piecing together of the narrative from various secondary sources, and the *a priori* use of common sense to try to give an interpretive meaning to the whole. Now for the Yoknapatawpha Saga there is no primary source material and only the secondary material of the novels. Or if it sounds better to say the books are the primary material and that nothing secondary exists, I won't complain. The all-important thing is that there's nothing else but the books. And they are works of art — this cannot be emphasized too much — which follow the rules, the forms of art, not of history. The result is that I am writing here a bastard product of art and history. Yet Yoknapatawpha county exists independent of either Oxford or the novels. How independent, we'll have to find out as we go along.

As part of the background immediate for the Saga are the names Yoknapatawpha and Jefferson. Yoknapatawpha is, as I said in the preceding chapter, the old name for the present Yocona River. The name is from two Chickasaw words — *Yocona* and *petopha* — meaning "split land." The name Jefferson, of course, is that of the famous Virginia statesman. But there is also in the actual Lafayette county, about ten miles east and slightly north of Oxford, a little country graveyard called the Jefferson cemetery.

Yoknapatawpha county is situated in northwest Mississippi. Its county seat is Jefferson, some seventy-five miles southeast of Memphis and forty miles from Oxford, the site of the state university. At the north of the county is the Tallahatchie River, and to the south is the Yoknapatawpha. A small section of pine hills is found in the southwest, above the Yoknapatawpha. The eastern half of the county, including the town of Jefferson, is mostly pine hills. The county has an area of 2,400 square miles.

In the *Collected Stories* Faulkner calls the group of tales in which the Indians appear "The Wilderness." And it is as a wilderness that Yoknapatawpha county first appears. For many years the Chickasaw Indians have lived here, having their own equilibrium with the forces of nature. We see them first about 1800, when the whites have already started to contaminate them. They are governed by an elemental code of justice and forebearance for the weaknesses of others. They are taciturn and cruel like the nature with which they associate so intimately. Race prejudice has never occurred to them, since a man's a man as he proves himself a man.

About 1800 the most important leader among the Indians is a vague David Colbert, who is described as being "the chief Man of all the Chickasaws in our section."[1] Within Yoknapatawpha county, however, the chief Man or chief about 1800, apparently less important than David Colbert, was Issetibbeha. He died and was succeeded by Moketubbe, his son. Issetibbeha's sister's son, Ikkemotubbe, became a friend of a captain of a trading steamboat on the Tallahatchie and went down to New Orleans with him in 1801. In 1808 he returned with a French friend from New Orleans and, by threat of poison, became the Man himself. Two years later he sold his son, Sam Fathers, by a quadroon from New Orleans, to his white neighbor, Carothers McCaslin. It was Ikkemotubbe, or Doom, who gave the square mile of land to Jason Lycurgus Compson in return for the speedy horse.

Another group of Chickasaws never too well related in the stories to the ones just talked about (in fact, in one place they are called Choctaws) is found in the story "Lo!" These Indians under the leadership of Frank Weddel, or Francis Vidal, go to Washington to get justice directly from President Jackson. Afterwards they agree to live

1. "A Courtship," *Collected Stories of William Faulkner*, p. 365. I am using the geneology of Faulkner's later stories about the Indians. His early stories contradict the later ones in certain details. Unless otherwise stated, all references to Faulkner's writings are to the first publication in book form.

west of the Mississippi River. A quotation from this story quite well introduces what is pertinent to know about the relations between the Indians and the whites. It is from a letter written by Weddel to President Jackson.

> Another white man came among us, to hunt in peace we thought, since God's forest and the deer which He put in it belong to all. But he too became obsessed with the idea of owning this ford, having heard tales of his own kind who, after the curious and restless fashion of white men, find one side of a stream of water superior enough to the other to pay coins of money for the privilege of reaching it. So the affair was arranged as this white man desired it. Perhaps I did wrong, you will say. But — do I need to tell you ? — I am a simple man and some day I shall be old, I trust, and the continuous interruption of these white men who wish to cross and the collecting and care of the coins of money is only a nuisance. For what can money be to me, whose destiny it apparently is to spend my declining years beneath the shade of familiar trees from whose peaceful shade my great white friend and chief has removed the face of every enemy save death ? [2]

In other words, the white man brought to the Indian the concept of property — of distinguishing between mine and thine instead of what is nature's belonging to all. And the Indian is thereby corrupted. Nature is the bountiful supplier to man, and man, through greed, destroys what nature has given him. The Indians did not destroy but were able to cooperate with nature for their own good.

That the land is regarded as bountiful by the Indians is clear. "This land for which, as Issetibbeha used to say..., the Great Spirit has done more and man less than for any land he

2. "Lo!" *Collected Stories,* p. 401.

ever heard of."[3] Yoknapatawpha county really starts its story with a generous natural bounty. Then the Indians enter and maintain that bounty, and finally white men — but their story of corruption is still unfolding.

The story of the whites in Yoknapatawpha county goes back to 1699. In that year Quentin MacLachan Compson was born to a Glasgow printer. Orphaned and raised by his mother's people in the Perth highlands, he fled to the Carolinas from Scotland with his claymore and tartan after having taken part in the sentimental revolt for Bonnie Prince Charlie in 1745 and 1746. In 1779 he fled to Kentucky rather than fight against the English king again. In 1782 his wooden-legged son, Charles Stuart Compson, who had fought for the British, but had been "attainted and proscribed"[4] by them, joined the old man, soon enough to bury him, at Harrodsburg, in central Kentucky. Charles tried to be a schoolteacher, but finally gave up to join General Wilkinson's conspiracy, whose chances for success were slim enough to attract the gambler in him. The conspiracy unsuccessful and Compson so unsuccessful a conspirator as to make his comrades afraid to have any association with him, he "fled by night, running true to family tradition, with his son and the old claymore and the tartan, still thinking that he really wanted to be a classicist schoolteacher."

Charles' son, Jason Lycurgus Compson, in 1811 rode up the Natchez Trace to the Chickasaw agency

3. "A Courtship," *Collected Stories,* p. 362.

4. William Faulkner, *The Portable Faulkner,* Malcolm Cowley, ed. (New York, 1946), p. 738. All quotations in this and the next paragraph are from the "Appendix," pp. 737-56; as a matter of fact, these two paragraphs are merely a summary of material in this appendix by Faulkner.

at Okatoba (probably a bit south of Jefferson because Okatoba is the name of the county just below Yoknapatawpha) and became a clerk to the agent there. Within a year he was a partner and winning large bets from the Chickasaws on quarter races. The next year, 1813, he owned a square mile of land "which some day would be almost in the center of the town of Jefferson." Here he remained to produce the Compson dynasty of Faulkner's Yoknapatawpha Saga.

Another family in the Saga begins with one born in the West Virginia mountains in 1807 [5] of Scottish-English stock. His family were poor whites, ignorant mountaineers, who moved in 1817 to the tidewater in Virginia. In 1820 he, Thomas Sutpen, ran away to the West Indies. There he married in 1827 a Haitian woman of part-Negro descent, whom he divorced in 1831 after she had borne him one child. In 1833 he showed up in Jefferson with money and slaves and acquired a large plantation. Just as the Compsons were distinguished by their propensity for staking all on the wrong side, particularly when it was a sentimental, seemingly glamorous side, so Sutpen was driven by a relentless ambition to be respectable and to establish his own family dynasty with the attendant traditions.

Another person from the Carolinas was Lucius Quintus Carothers McCaslin. He was born in the Carolinas in 1772 and died in Yoknapatawpha county in 1837. Aside from his relations with his Negro mistresses not much is told about him personally. His twin sons were Amodeus (Buck) and Theophilus (Buddy), who were born in the Carolinas in 1800.

Also from the Carolinas was John Sartoris, who

5. See the "Chronology" in *Absalom, Absalom!* for the dates of Sutpen's career.

arrived in the county about 1837.[6] Like Sutpen he already had money and slaves and stepped immediately into a prominent role in the life of the community.

These are the leaders of the county, but how about the mass of people? What were they like and what kind of life did they lead? They were a motley band — some coming for impossible-to-fulfill dreams like the Compsons and the Sartorises, some coming because of material ambitions like Sutpen, and the uneducated mass for combinations of these reasons and from the restlessness of the damned. They were "people named Gowrie and McCallum and Fraser and Ingrum that used to be Ingraham and Workitt that used to be Urquhart only the one that brought it to America and then Mississippi couldn't spell it either, who love brawling and fear God and believe in Hell."[7] These people made up the early population of Yoknapatawpha county, bringing with them the institution of slavery so that they could make more profits from the land and from their fellow human beings.

The origins of Jefferson go back to a Chickasaw agency and trading post, started shortly after 1800. Not until 1833 is the name Jefferson used or does the settlement think of itself as a town. The story of how the settlement became Jefferson is told in the preface to Act I of *Requiem for a Nun*. The process is one of "chance and accident."[8] Before becoming a town, the settlement

6. *Requiem for a Nun,* p. 44.
7. *Intruder in the Dust,* p. 148.
8. *Requiem for a Nun,* p. 4. The account, as being the most recent, found in this volume has been used as a basis for the story here, even though in other places, *Absalom, Absalom!* for example, there are variations. One of the problems in writing this chapter has been the different and sometimes contradictory versions of the same incident. As often as possible I have taken the latest

is pictured in these words: "Jefferson was not even Jefferson then. It was not even a town. It was a Chickasaw agency trading-post: a store, a tavern, a jail or calaboose, a half-dozen log cabins set in a disorderly huddle in the middle of the wilderness. ... There was no church, no school, least of all, a courthouse." [9]

Jefferson is already a Chickasaw trading-post when the three men who are called the founders of Yoknapatawpha county arrive from the Carolinas. They were Alexander Holston, Doctor Samuel Habersham with his eight-year-old son, and Louis Grenier, a Huguenot younger son. Doctor Habersham became the government Indian agent and his personality was intimately associated with the settlement. So close was this association that for some time the settlement was called by his name. By 1833 Holston, an old man, is running a tavern called Holston House; Doctor Habersham is dead and has been replaced by Doctor Peabody; Grenier is rarely in the settlement because he has become a very wealthy planter and has built a large manor-like house near what was to become Frenchman's Bend in the southeast corner of the county. He died in 1837 and Holston two years later. It is not until the twentieth century that descendants of these three men are mentioned in the Saga.

In 1833 the settlement becomes Jefferson and work is started on the courthouse designed by Sutpen's architect; it is completed six years later. Jefferson is flourishing. Ratcliffe's store gradually

version for my purposes. Sometimes the differing versions clarify an incident; sometimes they confuse. I have tried to avoid the latter.

9. "A Name for a City," *Harper's Magazine*, CCI (October, 1950), p. 200. This story was incorporated into the preface to Act I of *Requiem for a Nun*. However, the passage cited here was omitted.

becomes Ratcliffe and Compson's and finally Compson's. The mail is brought in by stage coach instead of by Pettigrew's riding his horse over the Natchez Trace. A girls' school, the Female Academy, is founded. The square around the courthouse fills with stores. The town grows.

Before the Civil War the cotton-slave economy was a prosperous one for the planters. Sutpen was able, with the help of his slaves imported from the West Indies and a French architect, to make real his dreamed-of plantation and erect his huge house. He married a girl from a genteel family in Jefferson so that he could found a Sutpen family dynasty. The Compsons became the leaders of Jefferson society, having their property both in and just outside the town. John Sartoris had his plantation four miles north of Jefferson. The McCaslins had their place in the northeast corner of the county. And in the extreme southeast corner there was Grenier's sprawling plantation. All in all, the period from 1840 to 1860 was the heyday of Jefferson's existence.

At this stage of our story the relations between whites and Negroes, though the Negroes were slaves, was a very intimate one, as the McCaslins illustrate in an extreme form. L. Q. C. McCaslin had as mistress both a Negro woman and his own daughter by her. The children of the masters and those of the slaves played and grew up together, except that part of the education of each was a realization of the master-slave relationship. Ringo and Bayard Sartoris in *The Unvanquished* were two such boys. Bayard learned that Ringo must sleep on the floor while he slept on the bed and was saddened by this awareness.

Another kind of insight into the minds of these people is afforded by the books in John Sartoris' library. Here were copies of "Coke upon Littleton, a Josephus, a Koran, a volume of Mississippi Reports dated 1848, a Jeremy Taylor, a Napoleon's Maxims, a thousand and ninety-eight page treatise on astrology, a History of Werewolf Men in England, Ireland and Scotland and Including Wales by the Reverend Ptolemy Thorndyke, M. A. (Edinburgh), F.R.S.S., a complete Walter Scott, a complete Fenimore Cooper, a paper-bound Dumas complete."[10] A library showing both intellectual curiosity and prejudices, romantic escape and practicality, learning and superstition. From such qualities was the civilization of Jefferson constructed.

The event which disrupted all this prosperity and equanimity was the Civil War. We never learn what were the attitudes of the people towards secession — war just happens and they take whatever part is assigned or is suitable to them. John Sartoris organized a company at his own expense and was elected a colonel of the regiment which went to Virginia in 1861. In an election the next year Colonel Sartoris was replaced by Sutpen and returned to Yoknapatawpha county to lead an irregular regiment of cavalry. Though little is told of his war career, Jason Lycurgus Compson II became a brigadier general and was always known thereafter as "General Compson." Henry Sutpen and Charles Bon went through the war with their strange relationship and tensions produced by forces much older than the war and outside it.

Within the county petty thievery and downright outlawry were frequent. Mrs. Rosa Millard (John Sartoris' mother-in-law) worked with Ab Snopes to steal horses from and trade with the Yankee

10. *The Unvanquished,* p. 18.

troops. This female Robin Hood outlawry was successful for a time but finally ended in Miss Rosa's death.

Jefferson was burned by the Union troops in the latter part of 1864. In one place it is said that Grant was the leader of the troops,[11] and in another it is General Smith who is held responsible for the destruction.[12] No details of the burning are given, and the event is treated very matter-of-factly.

Like all wars the Civil War finally ended, and the men returned to their homes slowly during 1865. One of them, Major Saucier Weddel — the son of the Indian leader who took his people to President Jackson to secure justice (in the story "Lo!") — was returning to his plantation in Mississippi, Contalmaison, through eastern Tennessee when he was killed by Union sympathizers living in the mountains.[13] Sutpen returned to find his plantation in ruins and tried to start all over again to build up a fortune but ended as a poor storekeeper. Even to keep store, he found it necessary to sell off most of his holdings and mortgage the rest. Something of the same story is true for most of the returning planters. General Compson mortgaged his square mile in 1866. And soon Reconstruction was on the community.

11. *The Unvanquished,* p. 159.
12. *The Portable Faulkner,* p. 741.
13. By way of historical explanation for the presence of Union sympathizers in eastern Tennessee, this state has always divided, and still does divide, rather sharply between the eastern and western halves. The mountainous eastern part is similar in many ways to West Virginia in its relation to Virginia. During the Civil War there were almost more soldiers in the Union armies than the Confederate ones from this part of the state. President Andrew Johnson's career illustrates this attitude. Today this division is an important factor to be considered in Tennessee politics, eastern Tennessee, for example, voting Republican as often as Democratic.

Reconstruction forces are symbolized by the two Burdens, grandfather and grandson from Missouri and out of New England, who were fanatical reformers and understood nothing of the problems of either the whites or the Negroes. An election took place for county officials which the Burdens in opposition to the people of the county under the leadership of Colonel Sartoris wanted to win. The two Burdens were killed by Colonel John Sartoris, and his friends won the election. This marked the end of the major efforts of the carpetbaggers to gain political control of the county. From then on, the town and county offices were occupied by Sartoris, de Spain, Benbow, and other old Confederate officers.

The economic struggle is another story. The carpetbaggers did win a partial victory here, but the townspeople fought back in the person of Colonel Sartoris. He managed to finance and get built a railroad running straight north and south through the county, through Jefferson, and past his own plantation. In 1874, with the railroad finished, he ran for the state legislature against his former partner in building the railroad, Ben J. Redmond (in *Sartoris* he is called Redlaw) and defeated him. Soon afterwards (in some stories it's the next day) on the streets of Jefferson, Redmond shot him and left town never to return again, thus ending the Reconstruction period for Yoknapatawpha Saga. [14]

The period between 1875 and 1900 is one in which the old leaders, such as Colonel John Sartoris, were either dying off or spending their time hunting and fishing and drinking. General Comp-

14. In *Requiem for a Nun* General Compson is a partner in the railroad operation, which is finished in 1876. The killing of Sartoris is dated as 1888. In the preceding paragraph I have used the chronology of *The Unvanquished*.

son died in his hunting camp in 1900. Sutpen had been killed by Wash Jones much earlier, in 1869, after Sutpen had seduced Wash's granddaughter and she had given birth to a baby girl. Isaac (Ike) McCaslin inherited the McCaslin lands and turned them over to his cousin McCaslin Edmonds. It was during this period that the wilderness made its last stand in the county, but it lost out to the men who were trying to make a profit off it by lumbering. Will Varner was getting his start in Frenchman's Bend. Gradually he got economic control of the district and acquired possession of the old house which had at one time belonged to Louis Grenier. In the nineties Jason Compson III's wife bore the four children — Jason, Quentin, Candace, and Benjamin — who figure in so many of Faulkner's stories. The father was rather deliberately and copiously drinking to get his mind off the unhappy present, his petulant, hypochondriac wife, and the idiot child, Benjy. The Negroes were either share-croppers on the farms in the county or doing manual labor or domestic service in Jefferson. A few descendants of the Indians were left, Sam Fathers being typical, the guide and confidante of those who went to hunt and fish each year in the camp owned by Major de Spain, located in a portion of Sutpen's one-time extensive holdings.

The children of the old leaders were proving themselves weak and ineffectual. Jason Compson III is typical of this decay. The tradition which produced John Sartoris, being sterile and unproductive, cannot meet new conditions or maintain itself in power. Each person has his own way of escaping the present. Mr. Compson has his alcohol, Mrs. Compson her illnesses, and Emily Grierson avoids the present by refusing to admit that 1920 is not 1890. Such escaping from the present inevitably produces in the individual various pathological psychic disturbances, and we therefore find those novels of the Yoknapatawpha Saga laid in the twentieth century filled with mental and physical failures.

Since the natural aristocrats (the Jeffersonian term here is particularly appropriate) of the community have abnegated their responsibility, who does take over the leadership? Ab Snopes was a bushwhacking horse thief during the Civil War. From 1875 to 1900 he and his relatives have been breeding children and moving as tenant farmers from one flea-bitten farm to another. Ab's son, Flem, about 1900 moved to Frenchman's Bend. The natural aristocrats failing to provide standards of values, any person who applies himself unremittingly to the pursuit of money and the power that its control signifies is a success. And that is the story of Flem Snopes, starting in Frenchman's Bend and eventually moving into Jefferson itself to become manager of the city electric plant and soon president of one of the local banks. Other Snopeses follow him and emulate his pattern of material success. Shrewdness and cleverness are now the ultimate standards of value, not standards based upon man's humaneness and humanity.

And so the story of Yoknapatawpha Saga since 1900 is one of the rather rapid decay of the descendants of the ante-bellum leaders and the usurping of their positions in the community by various members of the Snopes tribe. The rise of the Snopeses to power is the theme of *The Hamlet,* and numerous allusions to it are found elsewhere. The story of the decay of the descendants of the old families fills many books and is a story that fascinates Faulkner, since with this decay the rise of some such group as the Snopeses is inevitable;

so *The Hamlet* is a bitter, sardonic comedy and *Sartoris, Absalom, Absalom!* and *The Sound and the Fury* are tragedies of despair and frustration.

Turning from the general to the particular, the last of the Sutpens, in 1900, is a mulatto idiot, Jim Bond. The Compson family consists of the mother, the father, and four children. Quentin, the eldest, commits suicide while a student at Harvard, June, 1910; Candace, or Caddy as she is more frequently called, a woman who lives off her beautiful body, is last heard of as the mistress of a Nazi general; Jason becomes a clerk in a local hardware store and in his own penny-pinching, greedy fashion tries rather unsuccessfully to emulate the Snopeses; and Maury, or Benjy, as he was renamed, is an idiot who is committed to the State Asylum at Jackson in 1933. (Incidentally Jackson has an asylum for the insane, not a school for the feeble-minded. Faulkner was, I suspect, quite aware of this.) There should be added — to finish out the story of the Compsons — Quentin, Caddy's daughter. She, living with Jason and his mother, runs away in April, 1928, with a pitchman of a touring carnival and is never heard of again. The Sartorises in the twentieth century include Aunt Jenny, whom Faulkner is proud of and admires, as the title of the story telling about her death indicates, "There Was a Queen"; Bayard, the boy in *The Unvanquished,* killed in an automobile accident in 1920; John, Bayard's grandson, killed in 1918 as an airplane pilot in the war; and young Bayard, John's brother, killed in an accident while test-piloting an airplane in 1920, leaving a wife, Narcissa Benbow Sartoris, and a child, Benbow Sartoris. Ike McCaslin is a solitary widower, without children, who spends his time hunting and fishing and being a spectator of the events in the community.

The period 1920-1940, or the period between the wars, adds events even more violent. This violence is accentuated by the standards of materialism within our modern, mechanized society. Frequently Faulkner uses the airplane to symbolize this destructive, depersonalizing force. His novel, *Pylon,* though outside the Saga, is a study of the destructive fascination of the airplane symbol and as such fits into the entire pattern of the Saga. A novel, directly in the Saga, is *Sanctuary,* which uses the person of Popeye as the symbol of mechanical civilization and tells of his impersonal, though fundamentally impotent, destructiveness and the ineffectualness of Horace Benbow in trying to oppose that force.

The poverty-stricken, uneducated masses of this country produce the violence of fascist-minded leaders, well illustrated by the career of Percy Grimm in *Light in August.* Grimm is a kind of prototype of native American fascism with all its chauvinism, perversions, and sadism.

In the midst of these events the Negroes are in the town and the county, watching the decay and destruction about them. They maintain their roots much better than do the whites. As Faulkner has laconically put it in describing the character of Dilsey, "They endured." [15] The patience, kindness, and durability of the Negroes are the qualities that the whites have lost and now badly need. Lucas Beauchamp, descendant through the male line of McCaslins, is proud of his own individuality but in *Intruder in the Dust* patiently waits as two children and an old lady dig up the necessary evidence to save his life from a probable lynching.

The fundamental tragedy in the relations

15. *The Portable Faulkner,* p. 756.

between the whites and the Negroes is the difference in values. Neither group well understands the values of the other and conflicts, sometimes vaulting into grim tragedy, are inevitable. Perhaps the greatest tragedy of all is that of such a person as Joe Christmas in *Light in August*, caught between the two sets of values and unable to accept or be accepted by either group.

World War II has its effect upon the county. The draft before Pearl Harbor, being the work of outsiders, or outlanders, confuses the hill people like the McCallums, even though they have a very fundamental loyalty to the United States. But when they are told that they must go, they go, and participate completely in what happens. Others in the community also go, such as Chick Mallison and Benbow Sartoris, each to do whatever job is assigned to him.

So far, Faulkner has given us very little on the forties or the fifties. Only in *Knight's Gambit* and in a few scattered stories does he treat the events of World War II, not enough to develop a trustworthy pattern. All we can say is that the forties, in the Saga, are less violent than the twenties and the thirties. What the fifties will produce cannot be predicted any more than our own futures can be. And thus the Yoknapatawpha Saga for the present momentarily fades out but does not end.

IV

PARALLELS AND CONTRASTS

I now propose to compare Actuality with Legend and present the resulting parallels and contrasts. Then from these specific details and patterns we can see something of the significance of the relationship between the actual Oxford and the fictional Jefferson. I hope to see here what happens to the material that an artist works with in creating a work of art. Since the end products are works of art, we are on fascinatingly dangerous ground. It should be obviously true that we cannot see into the mind of the author, though we are trying to gain an insight into his creative methods by comparing his sources with his product. This round-about approach should tell us what we as readers need to know about what has happened to the raw materials of experience the artist has used in the books that particularly interest us for this study — and no more. I don't pretend to be omniscient, and whatever insights may be gained here are ones to be found from an inductive approach, not from any glittering generality that I might throw up in some regurgitative moment.

On a small scale our problem can be seen at work in the novel *Pylon*. In that novel Faulkner uses as his setting a metropolitan Southern city which he calls New Valois. New Valois is rather obviously New Orleans. I do not propose to go into the New Valois-New Orleans kinship here, since it is outside the scope of the Yoknapatawpha Saga, but the technique of transmutation is similar to the one we are concerned with. For *Pylon* the reader can place the geography and atmosphere of New Orleans against what is found in the novel. Faulkner knows and apparently is rather fond of New Orleans, having used it as a setting of another novel, *Mosquitoes,* in which Sherwood Anderson appears as the character Dawson Fairchild.[1] If one were writing an account of New Orleans in literature, Faulkner would be a major source.

Perhaps a good start in our comparative study is with statistics. First as to size — Lafayette county has a land area of 679 square miles; Faulkner gives his county 2400 square miles. In population — the 1940 census gave the actual county 21,257, of whom 8,573 or 40.3% were Negroes; the fictitious county in 1936 was given a population of 15,611, of whom 9,313 or 59.6% were Negroes. What do all these figures mean? Faulkner has apparently made his county large enough to include within it everything he wanted to throw in, though he is quite careless with his size. An example of this carelessness is the placing of Sutpen's Hundred in the northwest corner of the county, twelve miles from Jefferson. The 2400 square miles makes credible the existence of a hundred-square-mile plantation in one corner

1. There is some rather good criticism of Anderson as a writer on pp. 241-3 of *Mosquitoes*.

in a way that 679 do not. But the twelve-mile distance is off. It should be somewhere between twenty-five and thirty for a county with dimensions of about sixty by forty miles. If we take the actual county and measure off twelve miles northwest from Oxford, we find that we have a spot in Lafayette county corresponding to the position of Sutpen's Hundred in Yoknapatawpha county. The same kind of figuring can be applied to the location of the Sartoris plantation four miles straight north of Jefferson. In other words, Faulkner has said 2400 square miles as though he wanted the reader to think in larger terms, both literally and figuratively, than Lafayette county. Yet at the same time the novelist was thinking with the geography of Lafayette county and therefore used internal distances in keeping with its geography.

The population of Lafayette county has since 1870 varied between approximately 19,000 and 22,000. Faulkner gives his legendary county the number of people about half-way between the 1850 and 1860 figures. Why? Lafayette county in 1940 had 31.3 people per square mile, compared to a state of Mississippi average of 46.1 and a national average of 44.2 per square mile. Lafayette county is obviously a rural county. But Faulkner makes Yoknapatawpha county still more rural. His county averages 6.5 people per square mile — way below even the average for Lafayette county in its first census return, 1840, which showed about 9.0 per square mile. Yoknapatawpha county then must be thought of as a very rural and sparsely populated district. But at the same time we should notice that the life in the novels indicates a population density closer to 31.3 per square mile than to 6.5. The actual county is stronger in its specific influences than the abstract configuration.

Next — the proportion of white and Negro. Yoknapatawpha county has, as was pointed out before, 59.6% Negroes. The highest percentage of Negroes for the actual county was 47.5% in 1880 — always more whites than Negroes. In 1940 the actual figures just about reverse Faulkner's — 59.7% whites. Quite definitely the novelist has increased the proportion of Negroes. The immediate question is, of course, why? A glance at the Mississippi state figures may provide a partial clue. The high percentage of Negroes for the state was in 1900 — 58.5%. Since then the percentage has declined with each decennial census until in 1940 for the first time the Negroes were outnumbered by the whites (49.2% Negro). Is Faulkner taking his county back to a condition of 1900? Partially yes, but that's not the whole answer to our question. It is partially true in that the novelist sometimes confuses the past with the present in much the same way that his character creations do. But a second factor undoubtedly influencing the situation is the nearness of the Delta to Lafayette county. In the Delta the proportion of Negroes in some of the counties frequently exceeds 70 and 80 per cent. In trying to make his legendary county count for more than Lafayette county, the novelist has used characteristics intermediate between Lafayette county and the Delta. Another thing that this proportion in the fictitious county indicates is a psychological awareness by the inhabitants. They are so aware of the Negro's presence that it is as though there were more of them than there actually are. So Faulkner has given a kind of psychological figure rather than a physical one. Last but not least, the novelist may be saying that the presence of the Negro is his county's, Mississippi's, the South's number one problem, and the why for the "split land" of Yoknapatawpha.

I would like now to compare the histories of the two counties — Lafayette and Yoknapatawpha — that have already been given. It being easier to move from the whole to the parts, let's first look at the larger patterns of the histories. Here we find a very basic similarity. The countrysides surrounding both Oxford and Jefferson are alike; they were founded in much the same way and had settlers of similar origins. The pre-Civil War period is the peak for both. A destructive Civil War and Reconstruction is followed by the period between 1875 and 1900 during which the old leaders and the values that they stood for die a slow but complete death. Since 1900 each saw the rise to economic and political power of the red-necks and of the Snopeses. Industrialism is the modern goal of both towns. After two world wars we are in an uneasy present in both communities.

Within these large patterns of similarity the individual events and sequences of events take their place. As the first of these sequences, let us look at the Indians. In the earliest period the Chickasaw Indians are present in both the actual and the legendary counties, and they have as neighbors the Choctaws. That the Chickasaws were a great deal affected by the attitudes of the white intruders is shown by their taking Negro slaves with them when they left Mississippi for Indian Territory between 1830 and 1835. [2] Indeed

2. For an extended study of this particular problem see Wyatt F. Jeltz, "The Relations of Negroes and Choctaw and Chickasaw Indians," *Journal of Negro History,* XXXIII (January, 1948), pp. 24-37.

Faulkner has his Chickasaws, while still in Yoknapatawpha county, bothered by the problem of what to do with their Negro slaves. His descriptions of the Chickasaw character jibe with those given by such early historians of Mississippi as J.F.H. Claiborne.

The intimate relations between the French and the Indians (and this is more folklore than actual history) is found by comparing the careers of Doom, of the Yoknapatawpha Saga, and that of Greenwood Leflore with his French-furnished home, Malmaison. Malmaison reminds us of Saucier Weddell with his home, Contalmaison. One is led to wonder how closely the implied story of the Weddells, father and son, would, if made more explicit, parallel the story of Leflore, though Weddell is a Confederate officer and Leflore was a strong Union sympathizer during the Civil War. That Weddell is at one place made a Choctaw, as Leflore was, suggests that the novelist was directly influenced by the Leflore story.[3]

The difference in concepts of property between the whites and the Indians has frequently been noted by historians. Though Faulkner makes his own use of this difference of opinion, he is using material to be found in most historical writings about the Indians. Many people too easily assume that the property concept as found in our Western civilization is a universal one. The novelist is reminding us that this is not true, and that the confusions and misunderstandings over this difference are relatively recent in our own land.

The founding of Jefferson antedates that of Oxford by three years: 1833 to 1836. But much more important is that Jefferson had been slowly growing for the thirty years before 1833;

3. Faulkner tells some of Leflore's story in *Requiem for a Nun,* p. 106.

Oxford just about starts from scratch in 1836. Between 1830 and 1835 the Indians leave both counties. Faulkner makes this removal coincident with the naming of his town Jefferson. In Lafayette county the whites did not start active settlement until the Indians had just about all left; in Yoknapatawpha county the white settlements are started while the Indians are still present. The first thirty years of white pioneering in the legendary county is a process of infiltration among the Indians instead of the actual process of moving into unoccupied land. The role of the Indians in Yoknapatawpha county is therefore more important than in the actual Lafayette county. One device of Faulkner's for showing this importance is to have scattered Indians present in his county until about 1900, as in his story, "A Bear Hunt." In Lafayette county the 1860 census and those afterwards list no Indians. Undoubtedly there are present in the actual county, however, as in Yoknapatawpha people of mixed blood, especially Indian and Negro, like Sam Fathers.

Because the Indians have such importance to Faulkner, it would seem helpful and appropriate here to include a quotation about these Indians of 1900, who descend from the Chickasaws of a hundred years before. The scene of the story is just west of the Yoknapatawpha county line and that much closer to the Delta. As a boy Faulkner hunted and fished in this area.

> Five miles farther down the river from Major de Spain's camp, and in an even wilder part of the river's jungle of cane and gum and pin oak, there is an Indian mound. Aboriginal, it rises profoundly and darkly enigmatic, the only elevation of any kind in the wild, flat jungle of river bottom. Even to some of us — children though

> we were, yet we were descended of literate, town-bred people — it possessed inferences of secret and violent blood, of savage and sudden destruction, as though the yells and hatchets which we associated with Indians through the hidden and secret dime novels which we passed among ourselves were but trivial and momentary manifestations of what dark power still dwelled or lurked there, sinister, a little sardonic, like a dark and nameless beast lightly and lazily slumbering with bloody jaws — this, perhaps, due to the fact that a remnant of a once powerful clan of the Chickasaw tribe still lived beside it under Government protection. They now had American names and they lived as the sparse white people who surrounded them in turn lived.
>
> Yet we never saw them, since they never came to town, having their own settlement and store. When we grew older we realized that they were no wilder or more illiterate than the white people, and that probably their greatest deviation from the norm — and this, in our country, no especial deviation — was the fact that they were a little better than suspect to manufacture moonshine whiskey back in the swamps. Yet to us, as children, they were a little fabulous, their swamp-hidden lives inextricable from the life of the dark mound, which some of us had never seen, yet of which we had all heard, as though they had been set by the dark powers to be guardians of it.[4]

Jefferson, or Yoknapatawpha county, had three founders as did Oxford. The three in the fiction of Jefferson were Grenier, Habersham, and Holston; those for Oxford were Martin, Chisholm, and Craig. The detective-lawyer of *Knight's Gambit,* Gavin Stevens, is the last descendant of the three founders of Jefferson. But by a few years after the founding of the community, the three have disappeared from the scene except for Holston, who operated Holston House, similar to the inn and hotel run by Captain Butler in ante-bellum

4. "A Bear Hunt," *Collected Stories,* pp. 65-6.

Oxford. Martin, Chisholm, and Craig likewise disappeared from Oxford within a few years. Apparently they were ruined by the Panic of 1837.

To help make good on their investment of land, Martin, Chisholm, and Craig gave the county fifty acres to be used for the location of the county seat — Oxford. This fifty-acre site is in the middle of today's town. The nearest thing in Jefferson corresponding to the fifty acres of Oxford is the square mile given to Jason Compson I by Ikkemotubbe in return for the race horse. As the map on the end papers of *The Portable Faulkner* shows, this square mile starts from the center of town and, including the entire southeast quarter of the town, extends out into the country.

In talking about the origins of the early settlers of Lafayette county, I said that most of them came from Tennessee, Alabama, Georgia, and the Carolinas. Though Faulkner says little about Alabama, it is obvious that his early settlers followed much the same pattern. He does have Sutpen coming from the mountains of West Virginia via Haiti. Except for the Haitian background the rest of his early life would not have seemed unusual to the early settlers in Oxford. But the Compsons, McCaslins, Coldfields, etc. all came from the Carolinas and Tennessee in much the same way as Oxford's early settlers.

An event of some importance to these early settlers is contained in the phrase, "The year the stars fell," a phrase that occurs frequently in Faulkner's account of the early days of Yoknapatawpha county, especially in the novelette, "The Bear." This phrase refers to November 13, 1833, when a large awe-inspiring meteoric shower was visible over most of North America. It was apparently a more spectacular display than has been seen since because contemporary references to it are frequent and there are many allusions to it in the folklore of different parts of the country.[5]

The first impact of the outside world on Oxford was the Panic of 1837. In the Yoknapatawpha Saga this panic is never referred to. For Oxford, its ability to withstand the depression better than its neighbors, Wyatt and College Hill, for example, gave it a firm basis for its later prosperity in the 1840's and 1850's. Why does Faulkner omit the panic from his account? During the time of the depression Compson, Sutpen, and the other early land-holders were slowly but steadily building up their prosperous plantations. It suits his purpose that whatever difficulties they meet should come either from themselves, their neighbors, or the land itself rather than from forces outside the community. By ignoring the panic, Faulkner universalizes his account.

Picking parallels between actual people and fictitious characters is a fascinating parlor sport of criticism. It is perhaps most damning to the author when the fictitious character is a replica of the actual person. But it is interesting and meaningful to observe the starting points for the author's creations. Not only are events of actual history used as a basis for Faulkner's books, but actual people of Oxford's history have provided characteristics for his imagination to play upon and modify and change into something new. Sometimes all that will be used is a name. Lucius Quintus Cincinnatus Lamar is an example of this. There is Dr. L.Q.C. Peabody (whose physique and personality seem to be based upon Dr. T.D. Isom's), who figures in so many Faulkner stories of the early twentieth and late nineteenth centuries. And

5. For an extended contemporary account see "The Meteors of November 13, 1833," *American Almanac ... for 1835* (Boston: Charles Bowen, 1834), pp. 70-80.

there's Lucius Quintus Carothers McCaslin, first of the McCaslins in Yoknapatawpha county. And finally there's the dignified Negro in *Intruder in the Dust* and *Go Down, Moses,* Lucius Quintus Carothers McCaslin Beauchamp. He changes his name himself from Lucius to Lucas; so it is Lucas Beauchamp in *Intruder in the Dust.* With each individual the repetition of the high-sounding, resounding name reveals something about his character and becomes a symbol for the character's innate dignity.

As an illustration, among these early settlers of Jefferson, I would like to show the Oxford parallels for the career of Thomas Sutpen. The person in the actual Oxford whose career was most nearly similar to Sutpen's was Alexander H. Pegues, the first owner of Ammadelle, an antebellum house in Oxford. Pegues started in the late 1830's as a poor farmer and eventually became quite prosperous, owning four thousand acres and a hundred and fifty slaves. He also first lived in a bachelor hut made of logs. Not until just before the Civil War did he move to Oxford and start to build Ammadelle (the name was attached to the house by a later owner), whose architect, Vaux, had for Oxford such a French-sounding name. Pegues was also active in the new University of Mississippi and the local Episcopal Church, but that is outside our present story. Sutpen's character is obviously his own, but the events of his life are remarkably similar. The rise to wealth and power of the two is very much alike in its rapidity and completeness. Also, there's the source in actual events and folklore for the French architect made so much of by Faulkner. Though Pegues' house was in Oxford and Sutpen's on his Hundred, both had the desire for a kind of ostentatious symbol of respectability.

The rise to wealth of such individuals brings us to the peak of Oxford in the 1840's and especially the 1850's. Although comparatively little developed in the novels, Jefferson has a similar peak. Faulkner symbolizes this by making Quentin Compson II governor of the state during this time. The prestige of the Compson family is so great that its plantation is known as the Compson Domain. Uncle Buck and Buddy McCaslin are working out their ideas of social reform. Sutpen has built his house, married Ellen Coldfield, and had two children by her. Oxford had in the 1850's L. Q. C. Lamar, Jacob Thompson, Longstreet, and Barnard, each in the midst of a distinguished career with Longstreet near the end of his and Lamar and Barnard only at the beginning of theirs.

Some space was used before this to analyze the strengths and weaknesses of Oxford during the ante-bellum decade. In both Oxford and Jefferson we find a romantic sentimentalism; Sutpen's naming his horse Rob Roy is typical. The individuals who are the leaders of Jefferson illustrate vividly this romantic sentimentalism and the resulting potentialities for decay. The chief family is the Compsons with their veneer of classicism and tendency to gamble everything on the wrong throw of the dice of fate. Sutpen has his domineering, greedy passion for respectability, which he tries to attain by marrying into the Coldfields. Goodhue Coldfield (and how the man is completely characterized by the name) is a painfully respectably moral weakling and is only rescued from being a complete nonentity by his one-sided intimacy with Sutpen. Uncle Buck and Buddy are, by contrast, likable and desirable citizens, among Faulkner's truly great. Both Oxford and Jefferson have much the same strengths and weaknesses.

Their chief liability, even at the moment of greatness, is a self-destroying dependence upon resounding rhetoric, glamorous deeds, and ostentatious gestures. The novel *Sartoris* is a study of this fatally destructive tendency even into the twentieth century.

As a parenthetical remark, the pre-Civil War career of an actual person, General N. B. Forrest, is mentioned in "The Bear." In 1856 the McCaslins bought a slave from him in Coldwater, Mississippi, a town not too far from Oxford. Forrest was at this time a very successful slave trader operating out of Memphis, and Faulkner is quite right in using his name as a seller to the McCaslins. Forrest made enough money as a slave dealer (an occupation even in the South with overtones of non-respectability) to acquire that sacrosanct badge of acceptability, the ownership in 1859 of a large plantation in northwest Mississippi.

The Civil War was much the same kind of war for Oxford and for Jefferson. In Jefferson the inhabitants were probably more romantic about the war than they were in Oxford, but that need not be true. The war starts in about the same way — the University Greys being organized in Oxford (the Oxford of the novels is forty miles from Jefferson) with Charles Bon and Henry Sutpen as members of the company. Colonel John Sartoris has a war career paralleling almost exactly that of Colonel W. C. Falkner. Each man first went to Virginia as colonel of a regiment, was then defeated for re-election (Sartoris by Sutpen, Falkner by John W. Stone), and returned to Mississippi to lead a regiment of irregular troops for the rest of the war.

Life within Jefferson went on during the war in much the same way it must have in Oxford. Conditions were unsettled, but the women tried their best to keep the plantations running with what little help they had. Crime and outlawry were frequent, and one of the functions of Colonel Sartoris' regiment was to maintain law and order in Yoknapatawpha and the neighboring counties. As Oxford, Jefferson was burned by the invading Federal troops in 1864, though Faulkner makes much less of the burning than do the citizens of Oxford today. He does make the jail one of the few buildings left standing around the square after the burning,[6] though actually the present jail was built at approximately the same time as the courthouse in 1871.

Reconstruction took its toll of both Oxford and Jefferson. Some rather exact parallels are present. One parallel is the success of Lamar in 1872 in winning election to Congress and the election in Yoknapatawpha county in which John Sartoris and Drusilla Hawk defeated the forces of the Burdens, making both Oxford and Jefferson more successful in their counterattack against the forces of Reconstruction than were the average communities in the South.

Part of the Civil War and Reconstruction story of Jefferson is that of Colonel John Sartoris. It has become a commonplace of criticism to talk about the parallels between his career and that of Colonel W. C. Falkner, the novelist's great-grandfather. I have already pointed out the Civil War likenesses. What is also interesting is the post-Civil War career of Falkner. After the war he busied himself in building a railroad through Ripley, his home town, hoping eventually to reach the Gulf. Faulkner moves the railroad-building over to Jefferson and changes the date, 1857, of the building of the railroad through Oxford to

6. *Intruder in the Dust*, p. 50.

coincide with the story of his great-grandfather. The Ripley railroad was finished in 1872, about the same time that Sartoris' road was completed. Falkner and Sartoris were each killed by a former partner in the railroad-building venture. Each defeated the partner in an election, shortly after which the latter turned assassin. The killing of Falkner occurred in 1889, but for Sartoris this date is changed to 1874 to provide a better unity for the stories in *The Unvanquished* about him. The person who shot Colonel Falkner is supposed to have been R. J. Thurmond. The first time this story of the death of Colonel Sartoris appears in one of Faulkner's books, *Sartoris*, the man's name is Redlaw. Later in *The Unvanquished*, the name is Redmond.

The next series of fictional events, starting about 1900, is the invasion of the Snopeses into Frenchman's Bend and finally over the entire county. Here we find ourselves not able to relate specific incidents of actuality to incidents in the Saga. The Snopeses are symbols for a certain set of values and have only a symbolic relation to actuality. This is not to say that the symbolic function is not an important one and that the Snopeses and the incidents that occur to them may not tell us as much about reality as do characters and incidents forged directly from Oxford history. The Snopeses are one of the keys to an understanding of the effects of the twentieth century upon the lives of the inhabitants of Yoknapatawpha county.

By omission what I have said so far about the Snopeses as having symbolic function almost implies that they are the only characters of whom this is true, and this is not so. The Compsons, the Sartorises, the Sutpens — all have some kind of symbolic function in addition to the awe-inspiring individualism that they hurl against an unsympathetic world. No, in saying what I do about the Snopeses, I am not implying anything distinctive or unusual in their capacity as characters in the Yoknapatawpha Saga and the novels and stories. What I am saying is that their relation to actuality (and not reality) is different from the examples I have been discussing in the last few pages. The Snopeses are symbolic or representative of certain personalities and events in our present-day society, especially in twentieth century Yoknapatawpha county. These personalities are the political demagogues who, though unfit to lead, have taken over the leadership in modern society and act upon mercenary standards instead of human and humane ones.

Modern figures in actual Mississippi life who correspond to the Snopeses are Vardaman, Bilbo, and Rankin. These are the ones who exploit the new primary vote of the red-necks. Sometimes the new leaders are of the red-necks and sometimes they are not, but always they are exploiting the powers of the red-necks, after the old leaders have relinquished their positions in society. The Lamars and Thompsons are replaced by Bilbos and Rankins; the Compsons and Sartorises are replaced by Snopeses.

The World Wars, especially World War I, had a very important effect upon both Oxford and Jefferson. Both sent members of families to the war and some did not come back. Some who did come back are never physically the same again; others never mentally. The first war is a kind of psychic trauma and a means of escape for some people in Jefferson. Because, no doubt, of the importance of the disillusioning effect of this war in the life of William Faulkner the people of Jefferson are probably more hurt by it than the people of Oxford were. As yet there has not been recorded in the Saga any disillusioning effects of World War II, but perhaps later stories will provide that motif.

A particular event of the 1920's given in some detail in Faulkner's books is the Mississippi flood of 1927. Yoknapatawpha county itself, nor for that matter Lafayette county, is not directly affected by the flood, since the counties are in the hills above the Delta plains. But the indirect influence on Lafayette county must have been tremendous. Many people would have had either relatives or friends to worry about because the Delta is so near. In the Saga one half of one book deals with the flood. This is the "Old Man" section of *The Wild Palms*. Here the leading character is a Negro convict from the vicinity of Frenchman's Bend. This is made positive by the end papers to the Viking Portable selection from Faulkner's writings. The convict is in the state penal farm at Parchman, which is in the heart of the Delta ; so rather obviously he would be much involved in the flood. Even though the incidents of the "Old Man" are placed outside Yoknapatawpha county, the entire story has its place in the Saga as an account of a major event of Mississippi history affecting in so many ways the people of Lafayette county and by implication the people of Yoknapatawpha county.

Extremely important for Lafayette county yet rarely mentioned in the Saga, except in a few stories written during the forties, is the depression of the 1930's. In fact, the depression is almost conspicuous by its absence. During the thirties portions of Lafayette county must have approached Tobacco Road conditions. Though the university is a stabilizing influence in the town of Oxford, that is of little help to the farmers of the county. If the depression is so very important for Lafayette county, why is it omitted from Yoknapatawpha Saga? At the moment I frankly don't see what I think is a final answer to this question, but I can suggest various possibilities. My suggestions center on this feature of Faulkner's development, that the books which have as their theme a destructive despair were written in the early thirties. His writings of the late thirties and forties feature a much more nearly positive criticism of life than does the disillusioned romanticism, so strongly a part of Faulkner, of the early books. A possible explanation for this seeming change (change is really too strong a word) in his attitude is the influence of the depression in purging his own disillusioned despair and cynicism of the 1920's.

During the thirties a feature of Oxford's life was what I called its cultural renascence with the writings of the two Faulkner brothers and Stark Young and the work of the painter, John McCrady. Again this is omitted from the Yoknapatawpha Saga. The reason for this omission seems rather simple, since the author would then be giving himself powers of influence that he probably doesn't believe in. Also, that would particularize his presentation too much and distort some of the universalizing implications he obviously desires. Faulkner's critique of the South and the present day would be put out of focus by such an inclusion; so he omits it.

Though not directly a part of our historical pattern of Oxford, the life of William Faulkner the person has, as it does with all writers, affected the patterns found in his books. I am not referring to those unconscious subtle effects of an environment upon the way a man thinks, but to the direct employment by a writer of incidents from his own life. We see this particularly in the story of the Sartorises. Old Bayard Sartoris is a banker in Jefferson, who tries and fails to get his son into the bank after the war. Much the same thing happened to Faulkner in Oxford. His father was a banker, and Faulkner worked for a short time in the bank. Other experiences of his that appear in various books are his training in the Canadian Royal Air Force during World War I, and his interest in airplanes ever since; a sojourn during the winter of 1925-26 in New Orleans; various excursions to Hollywood as a writer (he has used Hollywood as a locale for one or two short stories); a trip to Europe in the early 1920's; and most of all, his many years in Oxford, Mississippi. It is amusing to note that, when Faulkner describes the activities of a character, Chick Mallison, in World War II, he uses terminology of the R. A. F., not the American equivalents of this war. He says "bomb dropper" for what Americans call "bombardier" and that pilot training consists of two stages, preflight and basic, as it did during World War I.[7] (During the last war we divided the training into preflight, primary, basic, and advanced.)

Besides the historical parallels, there are many geographical parallels between the actual and the legendary counties. A basic similarity is that Oxford and Jefferson are in the center of their respective counties. The two rivers at the north and south edges of Lafayette county are carried over intact to Yoknapatawpha county. The chief roads out of Oxford and Jefferson run approximately east-west and north-south. Diagonal roads to the corners of the county are also present in both. The railroad through Oxford runs more or less north and south as does the one through Jefferson.

7. *Knight's Gambit*, p. 240.

Most of Lafayette county is covered with pine hills as is Faulkner's county. The northeast corner of the actual county is part of a national forest that does not appear in the fictitious one. This perhaps would have brought in the fictitious county a too particular outside influence. The most conspicuous geographic difference between the two counties is Sardis Reservoir, not present in Faulkner's county. This reservoir was completed in 1940 and so could only have affected Yoknapatawpha Saga in the latest books about it. His not including it up to the present indicates a resistance to change which is part of his characteristics as a writer. As a person he apparently enjoys the fishing and boating on the reservoir as much as anybody, but it is as a writer that we are interested in him.

Oxford and Jefferson as towns present amazingly exact physical parallels. These parallels make us more easily comprehend such details in Faulkner's books as what is wrong at the end of *The Sound and the Fury* when Luster turns the carriage to the left at the Confederate monument on the square. Traffic around the square is one-way, and Luster is going against it, since the Oxford traffic pattern would demand that he go right at the monument.

The center square and the courthouse in the middle of the square are features common to both. The statue of a Confederate soldier is on the square just south of the courthouse for both. Even individual buildings have locations common to both Oxford and Jefferson. The county jail occupies the same position in both towns. Holston House is on the site of the old Butler Hotel, now the Colonial Hotel. For the sake of unity Faulkner has moved the airport up to the southern outskirts of his town instead of leaving it in the south part of the county where it actually is. Otherwise few changes have been made in the creating of the one town from the other. There's even the one weekly newspaper for both places.

The one exception is the omission of the university from Jefferson. Because in different stories he refers to the University of Mississippi, he finds it necessary to locate Oxford forty miles from Jefferson. The principal economic support of the actual Oxford is the university. So why does Faulkner so carefully divorce the town and the university? In having the state university on its outskirts, the actual Oxford acquires educational standards above those of the average Mississippi county seat, which affect the life of the community in many ways. By omitting the school, Faulkner makes Jefferson a more nearly typical community of northern Mississippi. He is here consciously universalizing his legendary region so that his books can acquire a wider meaning. How aware he is of the university's history is shown by a remark that it was founded in 1849,[8] only one year off. Faulkner is using, therefore, a device to make his books count for more than unusual tales of a particular geographic area. When the particular is convenient, he doesn't hesitate to use it and, in fact, seems to prefer to do so; but, when the particular interferes with wider implications, he deserts the particular.

Another kind of local material used by Faulkner in his novels is what loosely might be termed folklore. Some of this folklore is perhaps more accurately to be called historical trivia. For our purposes the distinction between folklore and the gossip of history, as Faulkner calls it, is not

8. *Absalom, Absalom!* p. 311.

important. What is important is the quantity of this material in his books. Since folklore is the elusive thing it is, it is hard to put a specific finger on too much of it, but we find it present in the speech habits of characters, in particular turns of events, and in the warp and woof of a book such as *The Hamlet*. But let me give a few examples.

I mentioned before the local gossip about a "French architect" for one of Oxford's ante-bellum houses. That little bit of gossip is apparently the basis for the development of the story of the French architect in *Absalom, Absalom!* A kind of historical trivia is the bringing of the seeds for a magnolia tree from South Carolina in a cigar box by the bride of Dr. T. D. Isom. This casual incident is expanded into the anecdote about Miss Jenny's coming to Mississippi.

> Virginia Du Pre had come out to Mississippi in '69, the last of the Carolina family, bringing with her the clothes in which she stood and a basket containing a few panes of colored glass from a Carolina window and a few flower cuttings and two bottles of port.[9]

Not that Mrs. Isom need have been the specific suggestion that Faulkner worked from, since such tales are no doubt frequent in almost any pioneer community; but, since the novelist knew the Isom story, the incident does show us a certain type of growth from actuality to the fictitious personality and event.

Another kind of folklore that has been utilized by Faulkner is the tradition of the brave, glamorous, Quixotic gentleman-soldier of the Confederate army. This is best illustrated in the story of Bayard Sartoris, brother of John, as an

9. "There Was a Queen," *Doctor Martino and Other Stories*, p. 99.

aide-de-camp to General Jeb Stuart. The story is told by Miss Jenny to a Scottish engineer in the presence of John Sartoris at the time when the railroad through Jefferson is being built.[10] There is no need here to retell the Quixotic story, ending appropriately in Bayard's death, since the flavor would be entirely lost in a summary. But it is true in Faulkner occasionally that the Civil War nostalgia is so real and strong as to make that war seem the most unreal of all wars.

I have already said something about Faulkner's use of names of actual people from the history of Oxford. Other examples of this besides the Lucius Quintus Cincinnatus of Lamar's name could be given. A casual visitor to Oxford will notice how many of the Negroes of the town bear the names of old families. The same thing is seen in fictitious Jefferson. An example is Isom, a servant in the Sartoris menage, named after Dr. Isom of nineteenth century Oxford. In the old records of the county appear a surprising number of the names familiar to readers of the Saga — Burden, Carothers, and many of the names of the people living in and around Frenchman's Bend. Even that mechanical symbol, Popeye, has his actual counterpart. There was in Memphis during the 1920's a gangster known popularly as Popeye.

The mention of Popeye brings to mind *Sanctuary* and the various incidents in it drawn from actual events. In Oxford I was told the story of two fellows who went to Memphis to study barbering and lived unknowingly in a brothel while going out to other places to purchase the favors such institutions afford. A version of this story is familiar to all readers of *Sanctuary*. Red's funeral in the speakeasy is alleged to have been based

10. *Sartoris*, pp. 10-19.

upon a funeral which took place in a Memphis roadhouse. Miss Reba is apparently based upon a well-known madam of one of Memphis' houses of the time. Feeding into *Sanctuary* is a great deal of Memphis lore and folklore in addition to the folklore of Lafayette county found in Faulkner's books in general.

David Kohn, writing recently about the Mississippi Delta, says that the Delta "begins in the lobby of the Peabody Hotel at Memphis and ends on Catfish Row in Vicksburg."[11] Remarks about the importance of the Peabody Hotel, such as this, are current through all northern Mississippi. In Faulkner this becomes a remark by Gavin Stevens:

> At the hotel... There's only one: the Greenbury. Did you ever hear of a Mississippian who has learned yet there is another one ? (Which was true enough ; there was a saying in North Mississippi that the state began in the lobby of the Greenbury hotel.)[12]

Such folklore and historical trivia in Faulkner's writings need to be illustrated here by only a few examples, even though almost innumerable ones could be cited. These sources have been for Faulkner very important in the creation of his novels and stories. The folklore and trivia provide a bridge between actuality and the legendary reality in his books. Faulkner attaches Yoknapatawpha Saga to actuality not only by tangible events and people but by the intangible, the seemingly trivial and unimportant.[13] Besides the folklore peculiar to his county (the distinction is fundamentally an

11. Quoted in Federal Writers' Project, *Mississippi,* p. 3.
12. *Knight's Gambit,* pp. 192-3.
13. For a suggestive study of the folklore in Faulkner's books see J. M. Machlachlan. "William Faulkner and the Southern Folk," *Southern Folklore Quarterly,* IX (September, 1945), pp. 153-67.

artificial one) he uses what might be called, in contradistinction, general folklore. For example, he frequently gives supersensory powers to idiots and the insane. Benjy in *The Sound and the Fury* and Darl in *As I Lay Dying* illustrate what I mean. Since this is a motif in folklore, Benjy's and Darl's apparently occult powers should not seem strange or out of character to the reader. Of course, the novelist does not depend upon such folklore; rather he makes it work for him and serve whatever needs he has for it. But, in doing so, he does not violate canons of actuality.

Just what is the relation between the actual world which Faulkner uses as his source and the legendary world he creates in his books? The parts of that actual world are the history, the social patterns, the geography, the historical personalities, and the folklore of Lafayette county. The parallels between these parts of the actual world and their corresponding parts in the legendary world have been already described. To understand the basis for the relationship between the two worlds, we must start with the folklore and historical trivia just discussed.

Faulkner employs a great deal of historical data in his Yoknapatawpha Saga together with a tremendous amount of folklore and legendary material. The kind of source which Faulkner uses is not important to him. Something of his attitude is seen in the following quotation:

> And what was it he [Howes] had been writing? Him, and Anne, and the poet. Word for word, between the waiting spells to find out what to write down next, with a few changes here and there, of course, because live people do not make good copy, the most interesting copy being gossip, since it mostly is not true.[14]

14. "Artist at Home," *Collected Stories*, p. 644.

"Gossip" — folklore and legendary material — is therefore basic to Faulkner's use of history. In fact, this gossip should be thought of as part of the historical material of actuality, of Lafayette county and Oxford, basic to the erection of Yoknapatawpha Saga.

In seeking what he is after, Faulkner does not want to be confined by literal, presumably verifiable truth. This process can be seen at work in his changing of dates from the Oxford story to conform to his purpose and needs in the Jefferson story. Statistics are, for him, one of the encumbrances to getting at the basic truth of a situation. Faulkner is almost indifferent to statistics — almost, not quite, since he wants his feet on the ground. Yet it should be kept constantly in mind that he has a tremendous reverence for history. The general patterns of history provide patterns for his work in a very specific way. What has been referred to as the historical sense of modern man is very much a part of the mind of the writer William Faulkner.

What is Faulkner trying for in this never-ceasing reliance upon history, either in its large patterns or in its minutiae? By now the answer to this question should be clear. He is trying to record the real history of a particular region of this country, using the material he knows himself and which is a part of him. No matter what factual and statistical divergences one finds, all the time he has fastened himself thoroughly on to the essence of the history of Oxford. He is trying to make the reality of Yoknapatawpha Saga a more real reality than the actuality of Lafayette county. Actuality is not ignored, because it provides the basic foundations upon which he builds his own reality. I intentionally do not say that he is creating a new reality, since the reality of his stories was also present in the actual county all the time. He is faithful at all times to what he regards as the true reality of the history of Oxford. To be faithful to the fundamental spirit of the actual Oxford, he finds it necessary at times to distort actuality. Truths may hinder one from seeing the truth. And it is the truth that he is striving for. We may disagree with his conception of the truth (or in more conventional jargon —his interpretation of history), but we cannot ignore this motive underlying his writings.

As evidence for what I am saying the changes in the story of Jefferson from its first telling in *Sartoris,* to the reappearances of some of the same situations in *The Unvanquished,* to a later restatement of the pattern in the Appendix to *The Portable Faulkner,* to the latest account in *Requiem for a Nun* are quite revealing. The name of John Sartoris' assassin is changed from Redlaw to Redmond as already described, and in *Requiem for a Nun* the change of date of the killing brings the fictional event still nearer to the actual event in 1889.[15] It is finally General Smith who burns Jefferson, not Grant. The Civil War in *The Unvanquished* is not nearly as glamorous and heroic as in the early *Sartoris.* Without using more details, I think I can safely say that most of the changes Faulkner makes as he retells portions of his Saga bring the Saga closer to actuality. The historical awareness is no longer something to be made use of in a casual, accidental fashion; it is the very essence of the Saga itself.

If Faulkner makes changes in his factual material to get closer to his concept of the history of the community, does that explain all the changes

15. In an early story Colonel Sartoris is still alive and mayor of Jefferson in 1894. "A Rose for Emily," *These 13,* p. 168.

that have been made? I ask this question, even though I am aware that the novelist is not basing his books upon careful, so-called scientific research, but is dependent upon what he has absorbed from living where he does and from being an extremely careful observer in his own casual fashion. I have said that certain changes from the pattern of Oxford increase the universality of the meaning of the Saga, and this universality becomes the second of our two imports of the Yoknapatawpha Saga in its entirety, the first being the Saga's relation to the actual history of Oxford. In so many ways, as we have have shown, Faulkner is faithful to his concept of the spiritual story of his own region in north Mississippi, but in other important ways his story is not just about a particular region but about the entire South, about modern America, and, at its greatest extensions, about modern man.

It is not entirely true that Oxford is Jefferson, nor is Oxford merely the basis for Jefferson. Both statements are equally valid and equally not valid. The forces of Oxford, Jefferson, and universality are not in equilibrium, nor are they always under the best of control by the author. At times universality takes over; other times the Yoknapatawpha Saga dominates the books; and finally and most frequently the spirit of Oxford seems to be the manipulating force. So thoroughly is the history of Oxford a part of Faulkner that not for long can he keep the activities in his books away from the activities of Oxford. Actuality intrudes upon reality. The actuality of Oxford history is the pervasive force throughout all his books. From that actuality the novelist has erected his reality of Yoknapatawpha Saga. In the books we may frequently find evidences of universality either through the use of literary symbols, his most common method, or through changes in the patterns of Oxford to make Jefferson more universal. But underlying all is his reverence for the essence of his community. And this is as it should be, since complete universality is merely a mathematical formula having only an abstract reality. The reality necessary for the author is one thoroughly saturated by actuality. And that is what we find in Faulkner's books.

His books suggest to us the legendary story of Antaeus, a son of the earth, who fought once with Hercules. Every time Antaeus was thrown to the ground the contact with his mother would give him renewed strength to continue the struggle. Finally Hercules in desperation held him aloft until Antaeus was exhausted. So it is with Faulkner. As long as he maintains his intimate associations with Oxford, he maintains his strength as a writer. It is in his deviations from the world of Oxford that he loses his strength. The texture that he contributes to his books is one derived from the texture of the actuality of Oxford. The more he deprives himself of his artistic roots, the weaker he is as a writer. No wonder he so frequently castigates people who for some reason are rootless in today's society.

V

HISTORICAL PATTERNS

We have seen that Faulkner writes his novels not as a scientific historian but as a person literally steeped in the historical lore of his community. He has consciously contrived and given to his readers a historical Saga containing the flavor and the spirit of the local history — this in spite of particular flaws or random contradictions. The Saga, whose existence had been implicit before, gained a concrete form in 1936, when at the back of *Absalom, Absalom!* a complete map of Yoknapatawpha county was published. Later, the Viking Portable selections supplemented the 1936 information. The elements of the Saga have been compared to the corresponding elements in the story of the actual Lafayette county. I propose now to move to the novels themselves and see what their historical patterns signify to the reader.

Before I do this I would like to explain just what I mean when I used the word "Saga" in the last paragraph. To understand the specific way in which I am using the word, we must look back over what has been said so far in this book. Our starting point for a comprehension of the world of William Faulkner was the actual history of Oxford and Lafayette county. Then we moved into the history of Yoknapatawpha county as it is reflected and implied in the novels and stories. Now I intend to have the reader look into the novels themselves. Notice the three stages in our progress: Oxford, Jefferson, the novels. The mind of the author starts with the actuality of Oxford's history, its gossip, its trivia, its folklore. Let us call that the first stage of his creation. Then from this first stage he has created a legendary county with a complete history. This is our second stage, a tremendous creative accomplishment. Finally, from this second stage, the Yoknapatawpha Saga, the author creates the third stage, what we read — the novels and the stories themselves. The Yoknapatawpha Saga as recapitulated in Chapter III is therefore only an intermediate stage, as I said before, one only implied in the novels. Faulkner does not write the Yoknapatawpha Saga; he writes from it. It would be patently naive to say that these three stages are in the mind of the novelist necessarily separate or in the sequence I have given here, but rather, what is more meaningful to readers is that they are implicit in all the stories and novels reflecting the Yoknapatawpha Saga. The creation and use of such a Saga is one of the great imaginative feats of the twentieth century novel. For this we should give to Faulkner our critical acclaim.

Like so many contemporary novelists (and poets and painters) Faulkner has been fascinated by the subtleties of craftsmanship. He has experimented with many devices, chiefly those within the traditions of the symbolic, subjective, naturalistic novel. These devices have been the despair of many readers and the joy of those critics who delight in the untangling of a literary puzzle. It is these devices which, added to Faulkner's particular stylistic mannerisms, have prevented him from having as many readers as he deserves. It cannot be overstressed that these nuances of technique are tools of the trade, not the finished product. With these tools Faulkner has become so adept that it is extremely easy to read him for nothing else, as many critics have. Yet there should be no doubt that Faulkner is one of the masters of craftsmanship in the novel of today, and it is as one of these masters that we now look at his works and ask a few whys about his techniques.

One could give innumerable examples of his facility and dexterity with technique,[1] but I will limit myself to one as an illustration of the relation of technique to literary form. *As I Lay Dying,* the author has said, was written "in six weeks, without changing a word"[2] — almost a *tour de force.* The novel is a folk comedy embodying tragedy, despair, and futility. These overtones are those particularly appropriate to Southwest folk humor, which has been noted for its violence and cruelty. Faulkner has applied modern subjective techniques to the violent material of the regional folklore. The basic story is the burial journey of the Bundren family, taking the body of the mother, Addie Bundren, who had requested burial in her family burying ground, from Frenchman's Bend to Jefferson. The husband, Anse, and the family take off for Jefferson to fulfill Addie's request and only arrive there after overcoming

1. For extended studies of Faulkner's techniques see F. J. Hoffman and Olga W. Vickery (eds.), *William Faulkner: Two Decades of Criticism*; H. M. Campbell and R. E. Foster, *William Faulkner.*

2. "Introduction," *Sanctuary* (New York: Modern Library, 1932), p. vii.

flood, fire, loss of a team, a broken leg, and their own mistakes — all this by people who exist on the same social and economic levels as the inhabitants of Erskine Caldwell's *Tobacco Road*. The problems of the individual members of the family remain with them, even though they are on such a journey, the novel ending with Anse getting a new set of teeth and a new wife; with one boy, Darl, on the way to the state insane hospital in Jackson; with another son, Cash, in the hospital in Jefferson, having his infected broken leg treated; and with the one girl in the family, Dewey Dell, showing her pregnancy more and more, trying to abort the baby, and wondering what she is going to do for a father for her baby — all this told through the stream of consciousness of the various participants, the point of view shifting frequently from one to another. This burial journey story is one found in many legends and tales since medieval times. Though I have been unable to locate the particular one, I feel fairly sure that what the author has done has been to start with the basic story in one of these legends, transplant it to Frenchman's Bend, and then present it by modern subjective methods. How closely the author stuck to an original story we can never tell until the hypothetical original has been found. Indeed it may very well be true that he was only following a general folklore pattern although his having written *As I Lay Dying* in six weeks leads one to suspect the existence of a more particular source.

The modern technique of the novel itself is the first thing that strikes the reader, and he is compelled by the author to see through it, and by means of it, to the underlying folk comedy, and then through that to the medieval or folk tale pattern. Using the terms already set up in this chapter, we recognize first the structure and technique of the novel, our third stage; then through these techniques we perceive the Yoknapatawpha folk comedy of manners, the second stage; and finally through all that has been already felt we discover the medieval or folk tale pattern, for this book the first stage. Difficult, yes, but the artistic effect of the whole is there, not in spite of these difficulties for the reader, but because of their presence. This novel is a product of a master craftsman skilled in the artifices of his trade.

The examination of all Faulkner's techniques is outside the discussion here, but I do want to explain one from which the other techniques derive or to which they directly relate themselves — the historical patterns present in his writings. To understand this, let us consider one of the central problems in the writing of history. This problem is that the events being narrated by the historian are usually familiar to the reader, at least in a general way. In contrast, a work of fiction usually has an element of suspense — the reader is curious about what is going to happen on the next page. The historian has not that advantage. If he is writing about the Civil War, it is not going to be anything new for the reader to find out that Lincoln was killed and the North won the war. Yet the historian is writing narrative almost as much as the novelist is. How does he create narrative suspense?

One method is for the historian to make his writing style as colorful, as dramatic, as vivid as possible. A good example is Carlyle's *French Revolution*. Some people have commented upon how drab and dull many twentieth-century histories appear beside those of the nineteenth, even though the later writers have had the accumulated benefit of an enormous amount of research. Carlyle, and he is by no means alone in using a second technique, as witness the currently being published *Teach Yourself History Library,* frequently centers his narrative for many pages upon the personality of some historical figure. Interest in the actions and character of the personality maintain the reading momentum for even a casual peruser. A third method is through the use of a specific interpretation of the events being told. Bancroft wrote how the events of American history had made this country a great nation and from those past events an even greater, more glorious future was to be expected. The finger of God was heavy in the activities of the American nation. Also, the writer of history may in his research discover little known or even completely unknown incidents and details of events whose telling adds much to the readability of historical narrative. The outline of the events may be known to the informed reader, but the details of those events may make for very pleasant reading. Scholarly monographs frequently depend almost entirely upon the presence of such details for whatever interest they may possess. Finally, there are at hand for the historian the principles that make any writing effective. By these principles I mean such things as clarity, conciseness, effective analogies (particularly valuable to a historian), and the employment of reasonable logic.

The methods of the historian suggest analogies to the methods Faulkner uses to create narrative suspense. A critical question about Faulkner has been stated by Alfred Kazin, among others, in this fashion:

> Yet why must everything in Faulkner's novels be raised to its tenth power? Why must the

idiot Snopes's love agony become "starspawn and hieroglyph, the fierce white dying rose, then gradual and invincible speeding up to and into slack-flood's coronal of nympholept noon"? Why must Rosa Coldfield's hatred of men become "that fond dear constant violation of privacy, that stultification of the burgeoning and incorrigible I which is the meed and due of all mammalian meat, become not mistress, not beloved, but more than even love. I became all polymath love's androgynous advocate"? Why is it that the Faulkner country must always appear as "a shadowy miasmic region," "amoral evil's undeviating absolute, " a " quicksand of nightmare, " "the seething and anonymous miasmal mass which in all the years of time has taught itself no boon of death"? For the same reason, as it must appear, that despite his extraordinary talents no writer has ever seemed so ambitious and so purposeless, so overwhelming in imaginative energy and so thwarted in his application of it. A fanatic, as Santayana once said, is a man who redoubles his effort when he has lost sight of his aim; and even if it be admitted that Faulkner's effort has been to express the inexpressible, to write the history of the unconscious, to convey some final and terrifiying conception of a South that seems always to exist below water, the impression one always carries away from his novels is of some fantastic exertion of will, of that exaggeration which springs from a need to raise everything in Yoknapatawpha County, Mississippi, to its tenth (or its hundredth) power because there is not sufficient belief, or power, or ease in his conception of Yoknapatawpha County, or the South, or human existence in general.[3]

And another critical discussion by Jean-Paul Sartre questions the use of time in Faulkner's novels. (*The Sound and the Fury* is the novel under discussion, but the same problem exists in so many of Faulkner's works.) Sartre finds that frequently the characters in the novels act as

3. Alfred Kazin, *On Native Grounds,* (New York, 1942), pp. 464-5.

though the acts they were about to do had already been done. His example is that of Quentin on his last day of life in Cambridge, Massachusetts, acting as though the suicide he was to commit had already been committed. That is, nothing happens; everything has happened.[4]

Can we, in the light of the historical patterns we have found in Faulkner's works, answer these questions? I believe we can. What is this raising of everything to its tenth power but an exaggerated form of the methods of those romantic historians of the early nineteenth century? Their techniques are those of dramatizing, of making events vivid and exciting, and of emphasizing individual personalities until the Tolstoian sense of the whole mass is completely lost. Of course, they had a different philosophy of history from that of Tolstoi, but that is not our concern here. If it be made our concern, we would have to say that Faulkner's philosophy of history is nearer the romantics' than it is Tolstoi's. Faulkner's characters act as though their actions had already been done, and that is identical with the problem the historian has in creating narrative suspense. The historian is writing about events whose outcome the reader already knows. Faulkner and even the characters in his novels treat events as though the outcome were already known. Granted that the writing personality of Faulkner must be congenial to this method and that Carlyle is out-Carlyled; still the explanation for these techniques of exaggeration and convolution is there. Faulkner has solved his problem of narrative suspense in the same way that the historian solves his. Because he is writing about

4. Jean-Paul Sartre, "A propos de *Le Bruit et la Fureur*. La temporalité chez Faulkner," *Situations I* (Paris, 1947), pp. 70-81.

Yoknapatawpha and not Lafayette county, he can and does increase this exaggeration so that the world in his novels is most decidedly his own world created by his own imagination.

Part and parcel of Faulkner's world are two things: Faulkner's disillusioned romanticism and the impact of early Southwest humor with its tall tales upon his world. Faulkner started out his writing career as an ultra romantic poet. His first volume of poems, *The Marble Faun,* published in 1924, is almost gushingly romantic with its fauns, satyrs, hawthorn, and nightingales. But Faulkner became part of the post-World War I disillusionment of Gertrude Stein's "lost generation." He read Eliot and Joyce faithfully and in writing about the world of actuality became the complete disillusioned romanticist even to the point of pessimism. In *Mosquitoes,* his second novel, he essays an attempt at the sophisticated table talk of the jaded intellectuals of the cynical lost generation. The novel is a failure, but it does indicate the trend of his thinking towards a cynical despair, even though he loves his land with a gripping, unceasing, brooding passion. This combination of cynicism towards man and love for the land produces the doomed fatality within which his characters have their being and only sustenance. Having this as their only sustenance, they inevitably react violently to such a rigid, inflexible determinism controlling their actions and existence.

The tall tales of early Southwest humor of the period 1840-60 affect the general techniques of Faulkner. I have talked about how important a part of his work is folklore and folk comedy as in *As I Lay Dying* and *The Hamlet.* In the first novel we have seen how the final presentation of the story is filtered through the folk comedy.

Characteristic of the humor of the old Southwest in such writers as J. J. Hooper, G. W. Harris, T. B. Thorpe, and W. T. Thompson and in such folk characters as Mike Fink are exaggerations (a tenth, even a hundredth degree do not seem too inappropriate), tall tale- or yarn-like flavor, rough and sometimes cruel horseplay, and a kind of love for nature and nature's direct gifts to man. Part of Faulkner's absorbed knowledge of his community would have been the old tall tales, perhaps even local versions of some of them. That Faulkner knows Southwest humor is specifically shown in *Mosquitoes.* He has Fairchild tell tall tales about General Jackson and his troops mounted on half-horse, half-alligator creatures. Later Fairchild tells a lengthy, involved story about sheep turning into fish, climaxed by a man's joining the sheep-fish and also turning into fish.[5] Here is a writer knowing not only the old tall tales, but also modern psychoanalysis (what reader during the 1920's could have escaped some acquaintance, no matter how superficial, with Freud, Ellis, and other writers on psychology?) and modern subjective techniques in the novel. Put these two types of knowledge together, start the writer to work writing novels, and what have you? You've got such a work as *The Hamlet,* yes, but more frequently Faulkner is writing tragedy than comedy. Transplant the combination of modern tall tales into tragedy, and haven't you got such a work as *Light in August* or better yet *Absalom, Absalom!*

One quite basic objection to what I've been saying is that the historian, or the teller of yarns for that matter, follows chronology much more than Faulkner does. To understand the impli-

5. *Mosquitoes,* pp. 66-8; 276-81.

cations of this objection, let us revert to our writer of history. There are narrative, chronological histories, and they are what we conventionally think of when we talk about history. But there is also the writer whom I will call, for want of a better term, the historical essayist — Toynbee in *A Study of History*. To compel such a writer to be chronological would be obviously meaningless.

Now turn to Faulkner. His books come nearer to being analogous to historical essays using the material of the Yoknapatawpha Saga than they do to being analogous to conventional histories. He violates chronology in much the same way that a writer about history, instead of a writer of history, does. It is not irrelevant that the historical essayist assumes a knowledge of the outcome of events as does the historian, as does the world of William Faulkner. Just as human history or some segment of that history is the necessary substratum for the historical essayist, so the history of Yoknapatawpha county is the necessary substratum for Faulkner's novels and stories. It is for this reason that I spoke of three stages in the writing of Faulkner's books: (1) the history of Lafayette county and Oxford, (2) the history of Yoknapatawpha county and Jefferson, and (3) the final novels and stories themselves. The end product is something which is not only about the other two, but it also includes them as pervasive forces.

So far the subject has primarily been the effect of these historical patterns upon the events and incidents in the books. What is the effect of these patterns upon the characters themselves? Upon Faulkner's concept of his characters?

What is important and revealing is the attitude

of the characters towards the past, and even time itself. The past is a vital force in the lives of all the characters and gives them a historical determinism of unremitting force. But let one of the characters give his own attitude toward time.

> It [a watch] was Grandfather's and when Father gave it to me he said, Quentin, I give you the mausoleum of all hope and desire; it's rather excrutiating-ly apt that you will use it to gain the reducto absurdum of all human experience which can fit your individual needs no better than it fitted his or his father's. I give it to you not that you may remember time, but that you might forget it now and then for a moment and not spend all your breath trying to conquer it. Because no battle is ever won he said. They are not even fought. The field only reveals to man his own folly and despair, and victory is an illusion of philosophers and fools.[6]

It may be objected that this is the statement by a character who is cynically drinking himself away from despair and into death; so let us have another type of character, Gavin Stevens, talk about time:

> It's all *now* you see. Yesterday wont be over until tomorrow and tomorrow began ten thousand years ago. For every Southern boy fourteen years old, not once but whenever he wants it, there is the instant when it's still not yet two oclock on that July afternoon in 1863.[7]

For the characters in his novels there is only what Faulkner calls *now*. But his *now* is more of a past including the present and the future than it is a present including the past and the future. To say the same thing in other words, the force of the past is so great that it permits only a present to exist, not a future. So the characters

6. *The Sound and the Fury*, p. 93.
7. *Intruder in the Dust*, p. 194.

struggle in their miasmal present, having no hopes for the future.

The historical awareness of the author governs very closely his choice of characters. No matter how highly individualized characters may be, they reflect part of the larger historical patterns. In this choice of characters lies one of Faulkner's greatest successes as a novelist. Not only are characters parts of the whole, but they are very much intrinsically themselves. In making fictional characters into parts of a historical pattern, a novelist can make them into types representative of the kind of people he finds in his historical sources or he can use individuals as symbols. The first Faulkner does not do too often, because the pull of the particular history of Lafayette county is so strong that individual characters are taken from that and then forced into whatever generalizations he wants their actions to indicate. As a direct result of this historical pull we find Faulkner more commonly using his individualized characters as symbols. Occasionally the drive towards symbolism is so strong that his characters become parts of what is almost an allegory, as in *Sanctuary,* but that is not usual. As symbols the characters, and even more important the actions of the characters, exist not only as literary symbols for the structure of the entity of each book or short story, but they exist as symbols of the strands in the entire Yoknapatawpha Saga. It is through this symbolism that the Saga acquires significance in more than the relationship of 2 to 4 and 6 to 8, etc. The force of the Saga is so strong that it should be admitted that it acts as a limiting factor on the choice of characters. Though characters acquire very stubborn mannerisms of their own, their selection is guided by the existence of the

Saga. This stubborn individuality is one of the sources for those minute contradictions we find among different novels and stories. That they are minute testifies to the author's control over them through the operations of the entire Saga.

The techniques of character presentation are suggestive in their relationship to our problems of historical patterns. It is impossible to say that these techniques are necessary to the characters, because, if the books were written in the nineteenth century with the same type of characters, situations, etc., they would not have had the kind of presentation they have. Faulkner is a product of the twentieth century and as such uses the methods of this century. These methods are the usual absence of the omniscient-narrator point of view, the talking about an event instead of giving the event, and a frequent use of the stream of consciousness technique. All these are characteristic of the post-Jamesian novel. These techniques obscure the social overtones, and the novelist gets around this by having some of the most long-winded, talkative characters in all literature. (Perhaps Conrad's Marlowe should be excepted, though it is interesting to note that Faulkner is a frequent reader of Conrad.) It is through this talk and the thoughts of the characters that Faulkner reveals the implicit relationship of his individual books to the Saga as a whole. The avoidance of the omniscient point of view prevents him from giving explicit relationships, but he can be as implicit as he desires.

The mention of social implications brings to mind how frequently in Faulkner we find the Freudian analysis of a character serving as social symbolism. *Sanctuary* is an obvious, perhaps too obvious, example of this. The novel has been psychoanalyzed[8] as an expression of man's fear of impotence, the castration complex. More exactly, the impotence of Popeye is to be seen as a symbol of a social impotence — the inherent destructiveness of mechanical civilization, which is impotent in that it cannot provide any source of values for man. Conventionally writers today use Freudian symbolism to connote sexual patterns in their characters. Here we find the sexual patterns of characters connoting social criticism.

The content of the Saga as a whole I intend to reserve for the next chapter, but it is appropriate here to discuss how Faulkner's historical awareness controls the content of each novel or short story. A first thing that a reader notices is how frequently it is true, as it should be with art in a satisfactory relation to life, that, aside from the literary interpretation of an individual book with whatever implications it might have, many interpretations of the life of the people in Yoknapatawpha county are possible. Differing socio-economic conclusions can be drawn, depending upon the material the reader selects. *Intruder in the Dust* is a good example of this. If one excludes from it the long discussions of Gavin Stevens on the white-Negro problems, one can use the material from the novel to prove that the Federal government should interfere by means of various anti-discriminatory laws, that the Federal government should not interfere (Faulkner apparently does not want it to), that the Negro possesses qualities greater than those of his white neighbors, and that the Negro is a member of a child-like, inferior race. There are enough of the variable, incon-

8. See Lawrence S. Kubie, "William Faulkner's 'Sanctuary'," *Saturday Review of Literature,* XI (October 20, 1934), pp. 218, 224-6.

sistent human qualities in the book to make all this possible.

Even though this intensely human quality is there, it should not be forgotten that the historical patterns of Yoknapatawpha county are the controlling factors in determining what incidents should go into particular books. The novelist is operating within a guiding pattern that both limits him and gives him a freedom of strength. If one wants to take the trouble with individual characters and incidents, one could rewrite all the novels and short stories containing material of the Saga into a chronological narrative, probably almost as long as the original books, but at least containing everything but the essential Faulknerian flavor. A suggestion of this possibility was made by Malcolm Cowley in his editing *The Portable Faulkner*. Particular incidents fall into their places in the Saga as a whole.

What is the relation between each individual novel or short story and the Saga as a whole? The Saga provides the author, via his extremely fertile imagination, with an almost inexhaustible source for incidents, characters, and all those things that go into the creating of a novel. The novelist selects what material he wants from the Saga on the basis of the artistic demands of a particular work. Yoknapatawpha county becomes a region upon which the author's imagination can play at will. Each novel therefore becomes the author's arbitrary selection from the material in the history of Yoknapatawpha county. It is in this process of selecting that the writer as novelist-craftsman comes out. The incidents in each novel are not selected on the basis of a chronological unity but on an artistic unity. Whatever objections a reader may have to violations of chronological order must be directed at the artistic whole of a particular book not at the concept of Yoknapatawpha county. As a result of Faulkner's particular methods the whole of the Saga is only implicit in each book not explicit. The reader must make his imagination work from the suggestions the author provides.

Since the individual novels are merely selections from the whole of the Saga, there are inevitably gaps. Though Faulkner's approach to his material is historical, his final moulding process is governed by his craft. There is no necessity for him to fill in the gaps unless he should feel a strong desire to do so. Particular gaps that might be pointed out are the period 1875-1900 ("The Bear" is about the only story set in this time); Jefferson between 1900 and the start of World War I (there are a few short stories about Flem Snopes' coming to Jefferson, omitted from *The Hamlet,* but that is all); the rest of the story of the Snopeses (for several years it has been rumored that Faulkner had two more novels about the Snopeses at the outline stage, but they've never been published. I have heard it said by friends of Faulkner that these novels will show that the second and third generation Snopeses have better qualities than did Flem and his grasping clan); the early history of the Compsons as outlined in the appendix of *The Portable Faulkner;* and the story of the three founders of Jefferson merely suggested in *Requiem for a Nun* and other places. I can see that making these suggestions has all the fascination of a parlor game, but there should be enough here to imply what I called the inexhaustible sources upon which the novelist can draw. What he'll do in the future is obviously his own business, but the presence of these gaps does arouse speculations.

VI

MORAL PATTERNS

In the last chapter I spoke about the intimate relationship between Faulkner's novelistic techniques and his historical awareness. Now I propose to talk about the moral ideas permeating his Saga. The objection is properly raised how such a discussion fits into this study, historical in its approach. To answer this question let us begin with what I have called Faulkner's historical awareness, which governs much of the manner in which he writes. How does it affect what he thinks concerning his beloved county? What is the nature of his historical sense?

It is a commonplace of historical criticism to say that there is no such thing as entirely objective history, no matter how many four-by-six cards the historian has filled out. There are always, in spite of sought-for impartiality, implied judgments. Faulkner is not writing a historical account of Yoknapatawpha county, but a critique of its history. Unlike most historians, he is not trying to avoid judging his county; rather he is constantly seeking new vantage points from which to judge it. To judge implies standards for judgments. What are Faulkner's? Almost always moral standards — not economic, social, or political.

It might be said that Faulkner uses his historical sense as a means of making his moral critique. Or again, the moral critique is used as means of making real the historical sense. Both statements are true and yet not true, because for Faulkner the two have become one and the same thing — his historical sense is a moral sense. To find out the nature of Faulkner's historical sense, we must examine the moral sense as revealed by his moral critique of Yoknapatawpha county.

A word of caution. Faulkner is above all a novelist. Don't expect, therefore, to find a carefully worked out system of ideas. Faulkner is just not that kind of writer. He is extremely perceptive in his insights into his own region, but those insights are a matter of emotion rather than rational deduction. This is not to say that the emotional insights may not be quite valid, even more valid than those of a powerful ratiocinative intellect. In fact, one of the things it is hoped can be explored in this chapter is the validity of his insights.

Because we are dealing with matter which is both historical and moral and we want to find the moral in the historical, the best approach would seem to be to follow the story of Yoknapatawpha county as told in Chapter III. That story starts with the Indians. Enough has been said to indicate what Faulkner's attitude towards them is and what they stand for in the Saga. The simple, uncomplicated virtues of the Indians are ruined by the white man and his placing a property or money evaluation upon nature and even upon his fellow man — the Negro slave. This is the moral flaw of the origin of Jefferson. These early settlers could have avoided this moral error by emulating the austere moral virtues of the Indians. But instead the Indians, before they leave the county, are corrupted by the concepts of the whites, so powerful is this moral flaw. Jefferson is doomed from its very beginning.

Before the Civil War the plantation-slave economy ruled Yoknapatawpha county. In spite of the moral flaw the planters did have a simple and fairly effective code of honor. This code in many ways is akin to that of Hotspur in *King Henry IV, Part I* and has the same weaknesses that Hotspur's had. The planters had a sense of justice, of honor, of decency, and of kindness to the weak. They were by no means perfect, but they tried to do their best. However they did not extend their code to cover their social inferiors or the Negro, beyond a patronizing condescension. The individuals who could rise above the limitations of the planter's code were few, Uncle Buck and Buddy McCaslin the only ones given. Thomas Sutpen's ambition was so strong that it both kept him below the code (not far) and made him successful in Jefferson until an outside influence — the war — destroyed his material gains.

The loss of the Civil War by the South is analyzed by Faulkner from the perspective of the flaws he has found in Jefferson before the war. As Miss Rosa Coldfield puts it:

> But that our cause, our very life and future hopes and past pride, should have been thrown into the balance with men like that [Sutpen] to buttress it — men with valor and strength but without pity or honor. Is it any wonder that Heaven saw fit to let us lose?[1]

1. *Absalom, Absalom!* p. 20.

The South lost the war because of its own moral weaknesses. If it had had a better code of morals, Faulkner, I am sure, believes that it would have won. He explicitly says:

> ... that day [Appomattox] when the South would realize that it was now paying the price for having erected its economic edifice not on the rock of stern morality but on the shifting sands of opportunism and moral brigandage.[2]

In the short story "Wash," Wash Jones begins to understand in 1869, when he kills Sutpen, why the South was defeated. He thinks of the Confederate planter-leaders — "symbols also of admiration and hope; instruments too of despair and grief."[3] Later in the afternoon, as he is awaiting the arrival of the sheriff's posse to arrest him for the murder of Sutpen, he thinks:

> Better if nara one of them had never rid back home in '65;... *Better if his* [Sutpen's] *kind and mine too had never drawn the breath of life on this earth. Better that all who remain of us be blasted from the face of earth than that another Wash Jones should see his whole life shredded from him and shrivel away like a dried shuck thrown onto the fire.*[4]

During this post-bellum period not only does Wash realize what is wrong with the old basis for existence, but the planters themselves realize it. They become aware of their own futility, and we find Jason Compson III drinking steadily and philosophizing much about the futility of life and time. Others seek different escapes. In *Sartoris,* where this tradition is most keenly analyzed though without a moral comprehension of slavery, we find Colonel John Sartoris realizing that death

2. *Ibid.,* p. 260.
3. "Wash," *Doctor Martino and Other Stories,* p. 237.
4. *Ibid.,* pp. 239-40. (Italics are Faulkner's.)

is the only way out for him. He has outlived his usefulness and belongs to a past time. On the last page of the novel is this paragraph (the use of the glamor and unreality of the Charlemagne mythology is revealing):

> The music went on in the dusk softly; the dusk was peopled with ghosts of glamorous and old disastrous things. And if they were just glamorous enough, there was sure to be a Sartoris in them, and then they were sure to be disastrous. Pawns. But the Player, and the game He plays... He must have a name for His pawns, though. But perhaps Sartoris is the game itself — a game outmoded and played with pawns shaped too late and to an old dead pattern, and of which the Player Himself is a little wearied. For there is death in the sound of it, and a glamorous fatality, like silver pennons downrushing at sunset, or a dying fall of horns along the road to Roncevaux.[5]

Even at its best the planter's code is a disastrous one. Perhaps in the time of Charlemagne it was suitable, appropriate, and good, but that time is long since past. No, Faulkner does not believe that the ante-bellum aristocracy represents the best possible for the South as do so many writers of and about the South.

The end of the nineteenth century witnessed in Yoknapatawpha county the loss of the planter's code and the values it stood for. The only values to take its place are the money values of the Snopeses. This is the tragedy of Jefferson today The time since 1900 has been one in which these money values have become more and more securely established. Modern-day materialism is the keynote of society.

Faulkner has used different symbols to represent this morally destructive force of materialism. Popeye is one; the airplane is another. In 1935,

5. *Sartoris,* p. 380.

the year *Pylon* was published, he wrote a magazine review of *Test Pilot,* a book by Jimmy Collins. I'd like to give a rather long quotation from that review, since it shows explicitly the meaning the airplane symbol has for him. Through understanding the meanings of the literary symbol, we can more easily understand the criticism he has of modern society.

> But this is not what I hold against the book. What I hold is that it is not what I had hoped for. I had hoped to find a kind of embryo, a still formless forerunner or symptom of a folklore of speed, the high speed of today which I believe stands a good deal nearer to the end of the limits which human beings and material were capable of when man first dug iron, than to the beginning of those limits as they stood ten or twelve years ago when man first began to go really fast. Not the limits for the machines, but for the men who fly them; the limit at which blood vessels will burst and entrails rupture in making any sort of turn that will keep you in the same county, not to speak of co-ordination and perception of distance and depth, even when they invent or discover some way to alter further the law of top speed ratio to landing speed than by wing flaps so that all the flights will not have to start and stop from one of the Great Lakes. The precision pilots of today even must have absolutely perfect co-ordination and depth perception, so perhaps, being perfect, these will function at any speed up to infinity. But they will still have to do something about a pilot's blood vessels and guts. Perhaps they will contrive to create a kind of species or race, as they used to create and nurture races of singers and eunuchs, like Mussolini's Agello who flies more than four hundred miles an hour. They will be neither stalled ox nor game chicken, but capons: children culled by rules or even by machines from each generation and cloistered and in a sense emasculated and trained to conduct the vehicles in which the rest of us will hurtle from place to place. They will have to be taken

> in infancy because the precision pilot of today begins to train in his teens and is through in his thirties. These would be a species and in time a race and in time they would produce a folklore. But probably by then the rest of us could not decipher it, perhaps not even hear it since already we have objects which can outpace their own sound and so their singers would travel in what to us would be a sound-proof vacuum.
>
> But it is not of this folklore I was thinking. That one would be years in the making. I had thought of one which might exist even now and of which I had hoped that this book might be the symptom, the first fumbling precursor. It would be a folklore not of the age of speed nor of the men who perform it, but of the speed itself, peopled not by anything human or even mortal but by the clever willful machines themselves carrying nothing that was born and will have to die or which can even suffer pain, moving without comprehensible purpose toward no discernible destination, producing a literature innocent of either love or hate and of course of pity or terror, and which would be the story of the final disappearance of life from the earth. I would watch them, the little puny mortals, vanishing against a vast and timeless void filled with the sound of incredible engines, within which furious meteors moving in no medium hurtled nowhere, neither pausing nor flagging, forever destroying themselves and one another.[6]

If the airplane is a symbol of materialism in its twentieth century form — mechanical civilization — can there be a more terrifying picture of what that civilization is doing to us? The values of Yoknapatawpha county have broken down completely and disastrously.

Faulkner's moral critique comes out most vividly when we consider one important source of his imagery — the Bible. Not only has the style

6. "Folklore of the Air," *American Mercury,* XXXVI (November, 1935), pp. 371-2.

of the Old Testament influenced his writing a great deal, but he constantly uses names, phrases, and other bits from both the Old and New Testaments. And this is particularly true in the novels most outspoken in their moral criticism.[7] The moral standards from which Faulkner is judging Yoknapatawpha county are those of the Bible, especially the Old Testament. Three of his novels, and just about his three best, where this religious imagery is most easily recognizable, are: *The Sound and the Fury, Absalom, Absalom!* and *Light in August*. That these three should be his best (perhaps adding to them that masterpiece of sardonic folk comedy, *The Hamlet*) and have the most religious imagery is undoubtedly more than coincidental — but let us go directly to the novels.

Let us examine before going into the Biblical influences in *The Sound and the Fury,* 1929, the book's structural difficulties, which, as we shall see, are not unrelated to the religious significances. The structure is just about identical with that of Eliot's poem, *The Waste Land.* What looks like a patchwork quilt of miscellaneous scraps is placed together by both men to form an emotional, artistic whole. The comprehension of Eliot's poem in all its levels demands a comprehension of his many literary allusions. A similar comprehension of Faulkner's novel demands a comprehension of the history of the Compson family given to us in the Appendix to *The Portable Faulkner,* 1946, "1699-1945 The Compsons." What literary allusions Faulkner uses are almost altogether to the Bible. The only exceptions are isolated references to

7. It is rather revealing that Faulkner is supposed to be working on a novel using the crucifixion of Christ as the basis for the story. See Carvel Collins, "Faulkner Story from a Novel to Come," Review of *Notes on a Horsethief,* by William Faulkner, *New York Herald-Tribune Book Review,* February 25, 1951, p. 8.

(Note: Since published as *The Fable,* Random House, 1954.)

Byron and Scott's Lochinvar. With *The Waste Land* literary allusions are not quite the right words since the implications of those allusions are fundamental to the basic theme of the poem, just as the Compson story is fundamental to Faulkner's theme. But the important consideration is that the primary techniques in the poem and the novel are identical.[8]

It is not only the technique of *The Waste Land* and *The Sound and the Fury* that are identical. Also identical is the theme of each. Each has its own individual modification and Eliot's poem is much more obviously inclusive than is Faulkner's novel, but the same pattern of the bewildered, wasted, degenerated present in contrast to the ordered past is there. The word *order* is even used by Faulkner in the last phrase of the novel, "Each in its ordered place." Of course, only the idiot Benjy senses this order, and the order is only one for an idiot. Both artists are trying to present a critical picture of modern man in his state of moral degeneracy. The cultural motivations that caused Eliot to write his poem are the same ones that caused Faulkner to write his Yoknapatawpha Waste Land. Just as one is a religious poem, so is the other a religious novel.

Let us look at more specifically religious implications in the book. Part one is Saturday, April 7, 1928. A carnival is playing in Jefferson and Luster wants to go but has no money. More important is that it's April, the season of spring and all that spring implies. As with Eliot, April is here a month for the dying and the degenerate. The second part goes back to June 2, 1910, the

8. Faulkner knows Eliot, as a reading of his second volume of poetry, *A Green Bough*, reveals. In *Pylon* one section of the novel is entitled "Lovesong of J. A. Prufrock." The *Collected Stories* has one section entitled "The Wasteland."

day before Quentin commits suicide in Cambridge, Massachusetts. June is the month of marriages; here it is the month in which Quentin thinks of his unconsummated incest and plans his suicide. The third part is dated Friday, April 6, 1928. This particular Friday is Good Friday, the day of the crucifixion of Christ. In the novel it is the day that Jason IV gives us his thoughts about what a hell of a person everybody but Jason is. He is shown cheating, lying, and being in general contemptible. The fourth and last part is Easter Sunday, April 8, 1928. Quentin IV has run away during the night with Jason's money and a pitch man of the carnival. Instead of the morning finding a Christ resurrected, it finds young Quentin out of the Compson tomb but in a very sordid present. Only Dilsey finds an awareness of traditional values through the Easter services in the Negro church. And her role is Tiresias-like in its quality of being a spectator of the Compson family degeneracy. Dilsey herself says after the church service, "I've seed de first en de last." On being asked what first and last, she replies, "I seed de beginnin, en now I sees de endin." [9] The Compsons are in the presence of the same set of traditional values that Dilsey recognizes but Jason is much, too much worried over the loss of his money to ever think about such things. As Jason says to Mrs. Compson on that morning, "You never resurrected Christ, did you?" [10] to which there is no answer, since the Compsons most decidedly have not resurrected Christ.

The character of Benjy adds much to these religious implications. On the day the story opens Benjy has his thirty-third birthday, making him the same age as Christ was when crucified. In-

9. *The Sound and the Fury,* p. 371.
10. *Ibid.,* p. 348.

stead of being crucified, Benjy is castrated (reminding one of the sexual imagery about the fisher-king in *The Waste Land*). Caddy makes Benjy's relationship to the Bible specific by saying, "Benjamin came out of the Bible."[11] She says this apropos of the change in his name from Maury (a family name of Mrs. Compson's family, the Bascombs) to Benjamin at the request of Mrs. Compson. Like the fisher-king Benjy is helpless to do anything about curing himself and is dependent upon the care of others. As Benjamin in the Bible is taken by the brothers to Egypt as a hostage for grain, so Benjy has a pasture belonging to him sold by the family so that his brother Quentin can go to Harvard and his father will not be deprived of his whiskey.

Light in August, 1932, continues this same Christ theme in the person of Joe Christmas. Joe first appears as a baby at the orphanage on Christmas Day (and is therefore given his name). Like Benjy he is thirty-three years old at the time of the novel. After being killed by the fascistic-minded Percy Grimm, Joe is castrated by his killer. The tragedy of Joe Christmas can perhaps be summed up by the phrase, "There is no room at the inn." For Joe there can be no peace in the world except in death, since he cannot be accepted either by the Negroes as a Negro or by the whites as a white. His final violent death is therefore inevitable and even more inevitable in its damnation of the world of the present which makes his death inevitable. Like so many of Faulkner's characters Joe is doomed from and by his birth.

Absalom, Absalom! 1936, takes its title from the Old Testament story of David and his beloved

11. *Ibid.*, p. 71.

but treacherous son Absalom, for whose death David mourned so deeply. The novel is the story of the rise and fall of the house of Thomas Sutpen. The story does not end with the death of Sutpen at the hands of Wash Jones in 1869 but is continued to 1910 (1909 is the right year but Faulkner uses 1910), when only an idiot mulatto descendant, Jim Bond, is left with the Sutpen blood. Dominating the entire book is the terrific ambition of Sutpen to found a Sutpen family which shall be respectable and strong. In pursuit of this ambition he is indifferent to the means employed and ruthlessly tramples on the people who might thwart his ambition. The events and people he tries to overcome eventually overcome him and finally destroy the family. The story is told by Quentin Compson to his roommate at Harvard, Shreve McCannon. He tells it at white heat, because Quentin is conscious of his own incestuous desires towards his sister, Caddy. Talking at great length about the possibility of some one else's incest makes him uncomfortably aware of his own desires. He is both afraid of and fascinated by the story he is telling.

In contrast to *The Sound and the Fury* and *Light in August* this book is almost sectarian, though the emphasis is still on the moral failures of Sutpen which produce the complete destruction of his dreams. In the other two books the values of the present are thrown against the values of the Bible and the present is made to look despicable in contrast. In *Absalom, Absalom!* the emphasis is completely away from the relation of man to God, and is entirely on man's relation to man. True, the same man-to-man relationship is the compelling force in *Light in August,* but the figure of Joe Christmas is bitterly contrasted with that of Christ. But in the later book Sutpen's moral failures are almost anthropological problems instead of religious ones (using *religious* in a rather narrow sense). Common to all three books is the moral scrutinizing analysis by the author of the society he has created. In all three Faulkner is a moralist lamenting the moral breakdown he finds, in much the same manner that Jeremiah laments the moral breakdown of Israel. It is for this reason that the moral analyses by Faulkner can be called religious studies.

Too easily it can be thought that Faulkner approves the institutional patterns of Christianity. This is not true. In *Light in August* the force which destroys Christmas, Hightower, and Miss Burden is institutional Christianity. Hines and McEachern are religious fanatics who make it impossible for Joe to ever be at peace with any world. They produce Joe's personal tragedy through their own blind fanaticism. It has been said about the situation in *Light in August*:

> Through Doc Hines, through Joanna Burden, through Hightower, Faulkner criticizes with penetrating irony religion which, shifting the responsibility of man's action from man to God, allows man to sink into abysses of social and moral degradation, into the sewers which Joe Christmas found everywhere. [12]

Faulkner himself says much the same thing about the people of Jefferson in the following passage:

> Pleasure, ecstacy, they cannot seem to bear: their escape from it is in violence, in drinking and fighting and praying ; catastrophe too, the

12. Althea C. Cater, *Social Attitudes in Five Contemporary Southern Novelists: Erskine Caldwell, William Faulkner, Ellen Glasgow, Caroline Gorden and T. S. Stribling.* Unpublished Ph. D. Dissertation, University of Michigan (1945), pp. 62-3.

> violence identical and apparently inescapable *And so why should not their religion drive them to crucifixion of themselves and one another?* he [Hightower] thinks.[13]

Churches are thoroughly damned by Faulkner. In *The Sound and the Fury* he followed the ideas of Eliot in *The Waste Land,* but in *Light in August* he rejects the Eliot of *Ash-Wednesday.* Eliot has found his order in institutional religion; Faulkner has rejected that and shown churches to be a destructive force in his county. What then is Faulkner's order?

What has been said so far indicates that Faulkner's attitudes towards his world are essentially negative. The novelist has been exploring human wrongs and telling his readers what a dastardly litter of people Yoknapatawpha has whelped. Out of this despair he has produced some of his best works, but is that all? Is there a positive side as well as a negative one? In 1931 Faulkner wrote a review of Erich Maria Remarque's novel *The Road Back.* The novel is a study of the problems faced by the veterans of the war when they return to their homes in defeated Germany. In the review he says at one place:

> It is the defeat which, serving him against his belief and his desire, turns him back upon that alone which can sustain him: his fellows, his racial homogeneity; himself; the earth, the implacable soil, monument and tomb of sweat.[14]

Out of the despair of defeat Faulkner sees man as turning to the things of elemental importance.

13. *Light in August,* p. 347. (Italics are Faulkner's.) This passage could serve quite well as an explanation of the amount of violence in Faulkner's writings.

14. "Beyond the Talking," *New Republic,* LXVII (May 20, 1931), p. 23.

And so does Faulkner turn to his positive beliefs out of his despair.

The starting point for his affirmation lies in his love of the land. The Indians in the Saga have more of this love than any other group of people, and this love is no small part of why Faulkner assigns them such an important role in his scheme of things. But it is not only the Indians who love the land; Faulkner himself is passionately in love with it. Only a man with an intense devotion to the things of the soil could have written this passage:

> Some Homer of the cotton fields should sing the saga of the mule and of his place in the South. He it was, more than any other one creature or thing, who, steadfast to the land when all else faltered before the hopeless juggernaut of circumstance, impervious to conditions that broke men's hearts because of his venomous and patient preoccupation with the immediate present, won the prone South from beneath the iron heel of Reconstruction and taught it pride again through humility, and courage through adversity overcome; who accomplished the well-nigh impossible despite hopeless odds, by sheer and vindictive patience. Father and mother he does not resemble, sons and daughters he will never have; vindictive and patient (it is a known fact that he will labor ten years willingly and patiently for you, for the privilege of kicking you once); solitary but without pride, self-sufficient but without vanity; his voice is his own derision. Outcast and pariah, he has neither friend, wife, mistress, nor sweetheart; celibate, he is unscarred, possesses neither pillar nor desert cave, he is not assaulted by temptations nor flagellated by dreams nor assuaged by vision; faith, hope and charity are not his. Misanthropic, he labors six days without reward for one creature whom he hates, bound with chains to another whom he despises, and spends the seventh day kicking or being kicked by his fellows. Misunderstood even by that creature, the nigger who drives him, whose impulses and mental processes

> most closely resemble his, he performs alien actions in alien surroundings; he finds bread not only for a race, but for an entire form of behavior; meek, his inheritance is cooked away from him along with his soul in a glue factory. Ugly, untiring and perverse, he can be moved neither by reason, flattery, nor promise of reward; he performs his humble monotonous duties without complaint, and his meed is blows. Alive, he is haled through the world, an object of general derision; unwept, unhonored and unsung, he bleaches his awkward accusing bones among rusting cans and broken crockery and worn-out automobile tires on lonely hillsides while his flesh soars unawares against the blue in the craws of buzzards.[15]

From the love of the land is derived what is so intense in Faulkner, the necessity for roots, or loyalty to one's region. The strength acquired by those having roots is frequently contrasted by Faulkner to the weakness of those without roots. In *Pylon* he uses this idea as one to characterize the fliers whom the reporter meets at the air races.

> They aint human, you see. No ties; no place where you were born and have to go back to it now and then even if it's just only to hate the damn place good and comfortable for a day or two.[16]

An individual acquires strength from his roots in a particular region. But this is true only when the region is a non-urban one and thereby provides that intimate association with the earth so necessary for a true sense of loyalty.

So much present is the problem of loyalties in Faulkner that it is interesting to compare Josiah Royce's *The Philosophy of Loyalty* with Faulkner's books. Royce has worked out his ideas about

15. *Sartoris,* pp. 278-9.
16. *Pylon,* p. 46.

loyalty into a logically coherent system, something Faulkner would never attempt to do. But there are many similarities between the ideas of the two men. Almost as though it were a commentary upon Faulkner, Royce discusses at some length how much more loyal a person is to a lost cause than to a winning one. As a matter of fact, what Faulkner senses rather intuitively and impressionistically, Royce has systematically worked out, though Royce's system is within a framework of philosophic idealism and Faulkner's impressions are not.

The group of people in contemporary Yoknapatawpha society whose love of the land, whose loyalties to the family and the social group are greatest is the Negro. Faulkner's attitude toward Negroes has changed a great deal over the years. The problem of the Negro in the South is becoming increasingly important to him; also, his admiration of the Negro is becoming greater. But let me give a series of quotations from his books to illustrate this. Talking of Negroes in 1927, he says:

> After all, only a few chosen can accept service with dignity: it is man's impulse to do for himself. It rests with the servant to lend dignity to an unnatural proceeding.[17]

In the quotation about the mule from *Sartoris* the Negro is the "creature... whose impulses and mental processes most resemble" the mule's. In 1929, the same year that *Sartoris* was published, Faulkner has Quentin Compson think about the Negro:

> The train swung around the curve, the engine puffing with short, heavy blasts, and they [a Negro and his mule] passed smoothly from sight

17. *Mosquitoes*, p. 11.

> that way, with that quality about them of shabby and timeless patience, of static serenity: that blending of childlike and ready incompetence and paradoxical reliability that tends and protects them it loves out of all reason and robs them steadily and evades responsibility and obligations by means too barefaced to be called subterfuge even and is taken in theft or evasion with only that frank and spontaneous admiration for the victor which a gentleman feels for anyone who beats him in a fair contest, and withal a fond and unflagging tolerance for white-folks' vagaries like that of a grandparent for unpredictable and troublesome children, which I had forgotten.[18]

Seven years later, in 1936, Miss Rosa Coldfield says about the half-breed Clytie: "A brooding awareness and acceptance of the inexplicable unseen, inherited from an older and a purer race than mine."[19] In 1942 Ike McCaslin is almost rhapsodic in his admiration of the Negro.

> They are better than we are. Stronger than we are. Their vices are vices aped from white men or that white men and bondage have taught them: improvidence and intemperance and evasion — not laziness: evasion: of what white men had set them to, not for their aggrandisement or even comfort but his own — ... .And their virtues — ... .[are] Endurance — ... and pity and tolerance and forbearance and fidelity and love of children — ... whether their own or not or black or not.[20]

At the same time that Faulkner is having Ike McCaslin say his bit about the Negro he writes this about the white man in his relation to the Negro:

> Then one day the old curse of his [Carothers Edmonds'] fathers, the old haughty ancestral

18. *The Sound and the Fury,* pp. 107-8.
19. *Absalom, Absalom!* p. 138.
20. "The Bear," *Go Down, Moses,* pp. 294-5.

> pride based not on any value but on an accident of geography, stemmed not from courage and honor but from wrong and shame, descended to him.[21]

White man's pride over the Negro is about as completely damned here as could be asked for.

I have already quoted from the novelette "The Bear," found in *Go Down, Moses.* A magazine version[22] of this story was published in the same year as the book. The magazine story is a fuzzy one about Ike McCaslin as a boy and a bear he didn't shoot. The novelette incorporates the material from the original version and adds a great deal to it. The theme of the final story is truth and justice, as in the short story, but this truth and justice is directly related to the problem of the land and the Negro. Ike, on attaining his twenty-first birthday, relinquishes his title to the family estate. This is undoubtedly a key story in the development of Faulkner's social ideas. He works out a social system here as nearly as he has yet done. In this system the important factor is the land. Ike repudiates his land ownership and, at the same time, assumes the obligations that the family ownership had produced. Part of these obligations result from the relations between old Carothers McCaslin and his Negro mistresses. Old Carothers and his two sons, Uncle Buck and Buddy, had intended, as Ike finds out on reading the family records, to maintain and make economically independent the descendants of Carothers and the mistresses. This Ike does as well as he can. He gives two of the three remaining descendants (he fails to find the third) a thousand dollars apiece and makes sure Lucas

21. "The Fire and the Hearth," *Go Down, Moses,* p. 111.
22. "The Bear," *Saturday Evening Post,* CCXIV (May 9, 1942), pp. 30-1.

Beauchamp's (one of the three) title to his little parcel of land in the midst of the McCaslin plantation is secure. Ike explains his actions to McCaslin Edmonds, his cousin, who assumes the ownership which Ike has dropped:

> I cant repudiate it. It was never mine to repudiate. It was never Father's and Uncle Buddy's to bequeath me to repudiate because it was never Grandfather's to bequeath them to bequeath me to repudiate because it was never old Ikkemotubbe's to sell to Grandfather for bequeathment and repudiation. Because it was never Ikkemotubbe's fathers' fathers' to bequeath Ikkemotubbe to sell to Grandfather or any man because on the instant when Ikkemotubbe discovered, realized, that he could sell it for money, on that instant it ceased ever to have been his forever, father to father to father, and the man who bought it bought nothing. ...
>
> Because He told in the Book how He created the earth, made it and looked at it and said it was all right, and then He made man. He made the earth first and peopled it with dumb creatures, and then He created man to be His overseer on the earth and to hold suzerainty over the earth and the animals on it in His name, not to hold for himself and his descendants inviolable title forever, generation after generation, to the oblongs and squares of the earth, but to hold the earth mutual and intact in the communal anonymity of brotherhood, and all the fee He asked was pity and humility and sufferance and endurance and the sweat of his face for bread.[23]

The brotherhood of man, which was emphasized by Hawthorne in so many of his writings, has now acquired the economic overtones of the "communal anonymity of brotherhood." But it is important to note the similarity between Hawthorne's and Faulkner's realization of the tremendous importance of the brotherhood of man. In such a

23. "The Bear," *Go Down, Moses,* pp. 256-7.

story as "Ethan Brand" Hawthorne shows how pride in intellect deprives a human being of what is most important — brotherhood. In "The Bear" Faulkner shows how our concepts of property are a violation of a God-given opportunity for brotherhood. For this reason Ike repudiates his title and goes to live in a little house in Jefferson.

How fundamental the role of the land is in Faulkner's thinking is shown in earlier (1938) remarks about the father and uncle of Ike McCaslin. That these remarks were made when they were shows that "The Bear" was the result of a slow, but steady, evolution in Faulkner's attitude toward his beloved land.

> There was more to Uncle Buck and Buddy than just that [ability at poker]. Father [Colonel John Sartoris] said they were ahead of their time; he said they not only possessed, but put into practice, ideas about social relationship that maybe fifty years after they were both dead people would have a name for. These ideas were about land. They believed that land did not belong to people but that people belonged to land and that the earth would permit them to live on and out of it and use it only so long as they behaved and that if they did not behave right, it would shake them off just like a dog getting rid of fleas. They had some kind of a system of bookkeeping which must have been even more involved than their betting score against one another, by which all their niggers were to be freed,·not given freedom, but earning it, buying it not in money from Uncle Buck and Buddy, but in work from the plantation. Only there were others besides niggers... .These were the dirt farmers, the people whom the niggers called 'white trash' — men who had owned no slaves and some of whom even lived worse than the slaves on big plantations. It was another side of Uncle Buck's and Buddy's ideas about men and land, which Father said people didn't have a name for yet, by which Uncle Buck and Buddy had persuaded the white men to pool their little

> patches of poor hill land along with the niggers and the McCaslin plantation, promising them in return nobody knew exactly what, except that their women and children did have shoes, which not all of them had had before, and a lot of them even went to school.[24]

"Faulkner implies throughout his novels dealing with the Southern family that social conscience, rather than social system, is the unattainable ideal necessary for the resolution of disharmony between the individual and society."[25] This is exactly right about the attitudes of Uncle Buck and Buddy. They have what Miss Cater has justly called a "social conscience." But in "The Bear" the fault is not only in the conscience of the individual but it is also in the economic system. I do not mean to imply that Faulkner has worked out a complete economic critique — not by any means. The social conscience of the individual is still all-important.

During World War II Faulkner published some stories giving the reactions of various people in Yoknapatawpha county to the events of the war. Some of the stories are merely light, entertaining ones about a family in Frenchman's Bend, the Griers. But in one of them he presents the McCallum family in conflict with the draft, or more exactly with an investigator the state draft headquarters has sent to Jefferson to find out what's the matter with the local board that the McCallums haven't registered. This is in the days before Pearl Harbor. The theme of the story is the weakness of the law in forgetting that men are individuals and as individuals are greater than the law. In the story Mr. Gombault, Jefferson town marshal, says:

24. *The Unvanquished,* pp. 54-5.
25. Cater, *Social Attitudes...,* p. 228.

> Yes, sir. We done forgot about folks. Life has done got cheap, and life ain't cheap. Life's a pretty durn valuable thing. I don't mean just getting along from one WPA relief check to the next one, but honor and pride and discipline [the Faulkner who wrote *Sartoris* would never have mentioned discipline] that make a man worth preserving, make him of any value. That's what we got to learn again. Maybe it takes trouble, bad trouble, to teach it back to us; maybe it was the walking to Virginia because that's where his ma come from, and losing a war [Civil War] and then walking back, that taught it to old Anse. Anyway, he seems to learned it, and to learned it good enough to bequeath it to his boys. Did you notice how all Buddy had to do was to tell them boys of his it was time to go, because the Government had sent them word ? And how they told him good-by? Growned men kissing one another without hiding and without shame. Maybe that's what I am trying to say.[26]

Faulkner believes that individual responsibility is the most important goal for man. Here is his positive answer to his own negative despair. An understanding of this individualism can be had if we think of Thoreau's individualism without the overtones of transcendentalism (how the two in Thoreau would be separated I'm frankly not sure). Thoreau is especially appropriate because Thoreau based his personal individualism upon his tremendous love of nature. In Faulkner the love of nature is replaced by the love of the land. How much one would want to distinguish between land and nature I don't know. Basically the only difference is again the transcendental ideas in Thoreau's concept of nature. Not being a systematic thinker of any sort, Faulkner's impressionistic reactions and demands for man do not carry him to the logical extremes of Thoreau's precarious position in his famous essay "Civil

26. "The Tall Men," *Collected Stories*, p. 60.

Disobedience." But it should be emphatically pointed out that Faulkner's individualism is not the "rugged individualism" of the social Darwinism of the late nineteenth century. Instead of having Thoreau's leaven of transcendentalism, he has Hawthorne's leaven of the brotherhood of man. Man must love the land that God has supplied to him for his well-being. Through the intimate association with land, man acquires a sense of loyalty to his family, his immediate social environment, and the all-encompassing land itself. Loyalties, as with so much of man's activities, are governed by what is inherited from the past. By accepting these loyalties and the force of the past, man develops his individuality — the end for which all the other things of man's existence are means. Undoubtedly by trying to make explicit what is only implicit in the novels, I may be presenting ideas that the novelist might be leary of, but their implicitness should be insisted upon.

In "Delta Autumn" Ike McCaslin is an old man going out for his November hunting for about the last time. It is now 1940 and Ike is seventy-three years old. To hunt, he must go two hundred miles west and south into the Delta instead of the thirty miles before 1900 to Major de Spain's hunting camp on the Tallahatchie. This loss of hunting grounds depresses Ike and he thinks about the Delta:

> This Delta. *This land which man has deswamped and denuded and derivered in two generations so that white men can own plantations and commute every night to Memphis and black men own plantations and ride in jim crow cars to Chicago to live in millionaires' mansions on Lakeshore Drive, where white men rent farms and live like niggers and niggers crop on shares and live like animals, where cotton is planted and grows man-tall in the very cracks of the sidewalks,*

> *and usury and mortgage and bankruptcy and measureless wealth, Chinese and African and Aryan and Jew, all breed and spawn together until no man has time to say which one is which nor cares....* No wonder the ruined woods I used to know dont cry for retribution! he thought: The people who have destroyed it will accomplish its revenge.[27]

But there is more to the story than Ike's depression with the present and nostalgia for the past. The basic problem of the story is love, and it very appropriately ends with the news being brought into camp that a doe has been killed by Roth Edmonds, whose Negro mistress appears in camp and talks with Uncle Ike. Early in the story there is this conversation between Ike and some of the hunters:

> "And maybe He didn't put the desire to hunt and kill game in man but I reckon He knew it was going to be there, that man was going to teach it to himself, since he wasn't quite God himself yet —"
>
> "When will he be?" Wyatt said.
>
> "I think that every man and woman, at the instant when it dont even matter whether they marry or not, I think that whether they marry then or afterwards or dont never, at that instant the two of them together were God."[28]

What can heal "this land" is therefore love, a love which must be so great that man becomes God. In this particular story the mistress, granddaughter of the James Beauchamp whom Ike had tried to find in Tennessee to give him his share of the McCaslin legacy, is strong enough to have the values of love, but Roth Edmonds is not. His not being so is not just a result of his own weaknesses but a result of social patterns and mores

27. "Delta Autumn," *Go Down, Moses*, p. 364. (Italics are Faulkner's.)
28. *Ibid.*, p. 348.

too strong for any one man to struggle against. The Thoreau overtones of transcendentalism in which man becomes God have become the Faulkner overtones of love in which man becomes God.

In Faulkner's latest novel, *Requiem for a Nun,* the problem of the individual is pushed further and the resolution is more explicit than ever before. The author picks a person about as despicable as one could find — the Temple Drake sitting in Luxembourg Gardens — and asks whether Temple's soul can be redeemed or made into something meaningful. The answer is quite definite — yes, through suffering. As Gavin Stevens says, "The salvation of the world is in man's suffering." [29] Temple must suffer for herself and her past. Nancy explains to Temple man's sinning and then suffering:

> You aint *got* to [sin]. You cant help it. And He knows that. But you can suffer. And He knows that too. He dont tell you not to sin, He just asks you not to. And He dont tell you to suffer. But He gives you the chance. He gives you the best He can think of, that you are capable of doing. And He will save you. [30]

Nancy's final words are that she believes, in what she doesn't know, but it is her willing to believe that gives peace of soul to her, a condemned murderess.

Quite rightly the publishers of *Requiem for a Nun* printed on the dust jacket of the book the section from Faulkner's Nobel Prize acceptance speech in which he says that man is immortal. The expository affirmation of that speech becomes the narrative affirmation of the novel.

Usually in talking about Faulkner's writings,

29. *Requiem for a Nun,* p. 276.
30. *Ibid.,* p. 278.

I have ignored any implications about his development and treated his works as a body of material from which I drew upon at will. But in discussing his ideas, I have been forced by the very pattern of his development to follow almost a chronological sequence. Since that sequence has been forced upon us, let us stop a minute and examine it. Just as I have divided Faulkner's ideas into the negative and the positive ones, so his development divides itself into two stages, the negative and the positive.

The first stage is what could be called his "Waste Land" phase. During this time the concept of the Yoknapatawpha Saga is developing so that in 1936 in *Absalom, Absalom!* a map of the legendary county is published and the county's history can be visualized in its entirety. The map, I might add, includes on it details about all the novels till then published in the Saga, not just those from *Absalom, Absalom!* This novel rather well marks the end of the Waste Land phase. As the quotations about the land and the Negroes from the various novels have shown, even in this period there could be found the implied love of the land, awareness of the role of the Indians in relation to that land, and a growing respect for the Negro. That he has this respect for the Negro early in this phase is shown by the character of Dilsey, by far the most admirable person in *The Sound and the Fury*. The later, positive stage should not be thought of as a sudden development but as a slow, steady evolution implicit from the beginning of the Yoknapatawpha novels.

The publication of *The Unvanquished* in 1938 can be used to mark the beginning of the new positive phase of Faulkner's ideas, even though some of the stories were published in magazine versions as early as 1934. Since those ideas are worked out so explicitly in "The Bear," this phase could be called his "Bear" phase. If *Sartoris* is contrasted with *The Unvanquished,* some of the differences between the two stages can be seen, since both books are about the same family, the Sartorises. In the first the novelist rather reluctantly admits that the Sartorises are self-destroying and that what they symbolize is not good for his county. In *The Unvanquished* Bayard Sartoris meets his father's assassin without making any effort to kill in retaliation. Bayard thereby acquires his "odor of verbena," or Sartoris tradition, even though he keenly realizes the flaw in that tradition and does his best not to allow the flaw to continue. The tradition of Roncevaux is found fatal in *Sartoris,* but not until the second novel is anything suggested to take its place.

As the first phase contains elements of the second, the second contains elements of the first. Yet, and this must be emphasized, these Waste Land elements are becoming fewer and fewer until we find the only vestiges in *Requiem for a Nun* are stylistic rather than ideological. In "The Bear" and other stories in *Go Down, Moses* Faulkner expresses his positive affirmation in terms of the land. We did find in "Delta Autumn" a vague insistence that love, in making man God, could heal the land. When we examine all the stories in this volume however, we are faced with the inevitable conclusion that fundamentally the author feels the land to be stronger than man. Man's destroying himself may be a means for the land's achieving its goal, the recovery of its original qualities.

Then we move on to the Nobel Prize acceptance speech and *Requiem for a Nun.* In the speech Faulkner explicitly refuses to accept the belief that man will merely "endure"; rather "he will prevail." Through what means will he prevail? One answer is in *Requiem for a Nun,* which assumes its place as a book very important in the development of Faulkner's attitudes. Man prevails and attains peace of mind through suffering. And it is man who has this goal, not just the land. His simple statement is, "I decline to accept the end of man."

Faulkner started his writing career as a romantic poet, quickly moved to disillusionment and despair, finally purged his despair and has now attained a belief in man. He has said to friends that he hopes the reader can obtain a catharsis from one of his books. Perhaps the disillusioned despair of the early 1930's served as Faulkner's catharsis and made possible his present belief in the dignity and worth of the human soul. To use Faulkner's own words, "The agony and sweat" produced "a spirit capable of compassion and sacrifice and endurance." As Americans, we should be proud of having a novelist who has gone from a negative despair to an affirmative belief without making the one too glib or the other too easy. Yes, the voice of the novelist William Faulkner is one of the pillars to help man endure and prevail.

APPENDIX

United States Census Reports

	Lafayette County		Oxford	State of Mississippi % Negro
1840	6,531	total population		
	13	free colored		
	2,841	slaves 43.5% of population		55.2%
1850	14,069	total population		
	4	free colored		
	5,714	slaves 40.6%		51.2%
1860	16,125	total population		
	7	free colored		
	7,129	slaves 44.2%		55.2%
1870	18,802	total population	1,422	
	7,983	Negro 42.4%		53.7%
1880	21,671	total population	1,534	
	10,286	Negro 47.5%		57.5%
1890	20,553	total population	1,546	
	8,853	Negro 43.1%		57.6%
1900	22,110	total population	1,825	
	9,730	Negro 44.0%		58.5%
1910	21,883	total population	2,014	
	9,904	Negro 45.3%		56.2%
1920	19,243	total population	2,150	
	7,963	Negro 41.4%		52.2%
1930	19,978	total population	2,890	
	8,236	Negro 41.2%		50.2%
1940	21,257	total population	3,433	
	8,573	Negro 40.3%		49.2%
1950	22,798	total population	3,956	
	8,023	Negro 35.1%		45.2%

BIBLIOGRAPHY

The basic source for this study is, of course, the books by William Faulkner which in whole or in part develop the Yoknapatawpha Saga. These are:

Absalom, Absalom! New York: Random House, 1936.

As I Lay Dying. New York: Jonathan Cape and Harrison Smith, 1930.

Collected Stories of William Faulkner. New York: Random House, 1950.

Doctor Martino and Other Stories. New York: Harrison Smith and Robert Haas, 1934.

Go Down, Moses and Other Stories. New York: Random House, 1942.

The Hamlet. New York: Random House, 1940.

Intruder in the Dust. New York: Random House, 1948.

Knight's Gambit. New York: Random House, 1949.

Light in August. New York: Harrison Smith and Robert Haas, 1932.

Miss Zilphia Gant. [Dallas]: The Book Club of Texas, 1932.

Notes on a Horsethief. Greenville, Miss.: The Levee Press, 1950.

Requiem for a Nun. New York: Random House, 1951.

Sanctuary. New York: Jonathan Cape and Harrison Smith, 1931.

Sartoris. New York: Harcourt, Brace and Company, 1929.

The Sound and the Fury. New York: Jonathan Cape and Harrison Smith, 1929.

These 13. New York: Jonathan Cape and Harrison Smith, 1931.

The Unvanquished. New York: Random House, 1938.

The Wild Palms. New York: Random House, 1939.

For its special importance in helping the reader of Faulkner understand the Yoknapatawpha Saga the following selection from the works should be mentioned: Malcolm Cowley (ed.), *The Portable Faulkner*. New York: Viking Press, 1946.

The most important bibliographic account of writings by Faulkner is: Robert W. Daniel, *A Catalogue of the Writings of William Faulkner*. New Haven: Yale University Library, 1942. The most recent and most complete bibliography of criticism on Faulkner is found in Frederick J. Hoffman and Olga W. Vickery (eds.), *William Faulkner: Two Decades of Criticism*. East Lansing, Mich.: Michigan State College Press, 1951. Pages 269-280. One book, not included in this bibliography, should be added: Harry M. Campbell and Ruel E. Foster, *William Faulkner: A Critical Appraisal*. Norman, Okla.: University of Oklahoma Press, 1951.

The history of Oxford, Mississippi, and Lafayette county has been one that I have had to piece together from here and there. My principal sources have been:

Belcher, John C. and King, Morton B. Jr. *Mississippi's People*. University, Miss.: University of Mississippi, 1950.

Bettersworth, John K. *Confederate Mississippi, the People and Policies of a Cotton State in Wartime*. Baton Rouge: Louisiana State University Press, 1943.

Cabaniss, James A. *A History of the University of Mississippi*. University, Miss.: University of Mississippi, 1949.

Campbell, Florence E. (ed.) *Journal of the Minutes of the Board of Trustees of the University of Mississippi 1845-1860.* M.A. Thesis. University of Mississippi, 1939.

Claiborne, John F. H. *Mississippi as a Province, Territory and State.* Jackson, Miss.: Power and Barksdale, 1880.

Cole, James D. *Origin of the White Population of Lafayette County.* M.A. Thesis. University of Mississippi, 1935.

Davis, Reuben. *Recollections of Mississippi and Mississippians.* Boston: Houghton Mifflin, 1889.

Evans, Medford. "Oxford, Mississippi." *Southwest Review,* XV (October, 1929), 46-63.

Federal Writers' Project. *Mississippi; a Guide to the* Magnolia State. New York: Viking Press, 1938.

Garner, J. W. *Reconstruction in Mississippi.* New York: Macmillan, 1901.

Hathorn, John C. *A Period Study of Lafayette County from 1836 to 1860 with Emphasis on Population Groups.* M.A. Thesis. University of Mississippi, 1939.

Hearon, Cleo C. *Mississippi and the Compromise of 1850.* Oxford, Miss.: Mississippi Historical Society, 1913.

Historical Catalogue of the University of Mississippi, 1849-1909. Nashville: Marshall and Bruce Company, 1910.

Holt, Mrs. Minnie Smith. "Oxford, Mississippi." MS. University of Mississippi Library, [1936].

Johnson, Jemmy Grant. "The Civil War Hospital at the University." *Publications of the Mississippi Historical Society,* XII, 94-106.

Kendel, Julia. "Reconstruction in Lafayette County." *Publications of the Mississippi Historical Society,* XIII, 223-271.

Mayes, Edward. *History of Education in Mississippi.* Washington: Government Printing Office, 1899.

Mayes, Edward. *Lucius Q. C. Lamar: His Life, Times, and Speeches.* Nashville: Publishing House of the Methodist Episcopal Church, South, 1896.

Rainwater, Percy Lee. *Mississippi, Storm Center of Secession, 1856-1861.* Baton Rouge: O. Claitor, 1938.

Rowland, Dunbar. *Mississippi: the Heart of the South.* 2 vols. Chicago: S. J. Clarke, 1925.

"Some Early History of Lafayette County, Mississippi." Compiled by David Reese Chapter D. A. R. Begun in October 1922. MS. University of Mississippi Library.

Sydnor, Charles Sackett. *Slavery in Mississippi.* New York: Appleton-Century, 1933.

Early manuscript records of Lafayette county are to be found in the offices of the clerk of circuit court and the clerk of chancery court, Courthouse, Oxford, Mississippi. Some miscellaneous records and relics are in the Mary Buie Museum in Oxford. The manuscript records and notes made by WPA workers concerning Lafayette county, which are in the State Archives, Jackson, Mississippi, are quite valuable. Also in the State Archives are files of the old newspapers of Oxford.

INDEX